MASTER
MANIPULATORS

DISCOVER COVERT TACTICS
NARCISSISTS DEVISE TO MANIPULATE, DECEIVE, AND
CONTROL

LYNN NICHOLS

Master Manipulators: Discover Covert Tactics Narcissists Devise to Manipulate, Deceive, and Control

Author: Lynn Nichols

Published by: Link Media Group, LLC

Moving Forward with Hope, Website: https://movingforwardafterabuse.com/

Email: info@movingforwardafterabuse.com

National Domestic Violence Hotline 1-800-799-7233 (English)/1-800-797-3224 (En Español)

A SPECIAL BONUS

Thank you for purchasing this book.

I want to encourage you on your journey if you are overcoming emotional abuse from toxic individual(s) by sending to you a Free eBook, called:

49 POWERHOUSE AFFIRMATIONS: Rejuvenate your Soul and Mind after a Destructive Relationship

It's a downloadable eBook, and about 55 pages. We want to provide as our way of saying thank you and to provide encouragement on your journey.

Click Here to Claim Your Free Copy:

A Special Note

When we are exiting an emotionally abusive situation, we may be downtrodden, feel lost and be discouraged by our situation.

I have been there.

Maybe you have gone no contact, or grey rock with someone, these times can leave us feeling a bit empty. Sometimes, there is no one to cheer us along on the journey to freedom, especially at the onset. There are many emotions, that seem to come together at the same time, and it can be a confusing time.

These affirmations are geared to uplift, encourage, and serve as a tool to empower us to see how far we have come, call out what we have endured, and to be strengthened by it. We are able to move forward, when ready, and at a time that is right for us.

Affirmations have been written, for the most part, in first person singular, however feel free to adjust accordingly.

Some of these affirmations are deep and need to be digested and thought about for some time. While this book can be read is a very short time span, the intent is to realize that we are different than what the abuser/manipulators told us. It takes time to separate the lies, from the truth.

<u>Click Here to Claim Your Free Copy:</u>

49 POWERHOUSE AFFIRMATIONS

Table of Contents

PREFACE

Sometimes, some knowledge is too deep, too hard to hear, we choose to ignore it for days, weeks, or decades, but we know it's right. Sometimes there is a message within us that we try to run from, then come back to it, only to finally share it. I have fought with this message, re-written this manuscript several times, to convey what is in my heart based on experiential knowledge coupled with the research I've compiled for several years now.

I'm giving my message a voice.

I am not an expert on this subject, though sometimes I feel like I have inadvertently become one, an experience I did not intend to write about.

I do not have a PHD, am not a psychologist, therapist, or a counselor. I write based on my years of personal experience and research that I have gathered in my attempt to understand what was happening in my marriage and family relationships, to include close friendships, so that you can have your experiences validated, and start to rebuild if you deem it be the right move for you.

I have had several light bulb moments in my own journey in recovering from narcissistic abuse. There may be others that may be impacted by the same issues which we will outline in this book.

I love people, have a heart of empathy, and hope to be a beacon of light in this age where manipulation and a covert agenda is common; bringing light to this topic burns in my heart.

My first introductory book, <u>Overcoming the Devastation of Narcissistic Abuse: How to Heal, Recover and Take Your Life Back</u> was released in 2018. Overcoming the Devastation of Narcissistic Abuse, begins the journey to move forward to make the right changes to heal and recover as an introductory guidebook.

There are many people who have been impacted by manipulators, and like me, are moving forward on the path to be an overcomer from the devastating trail that was left behind. It is a journey, and the road to recovery does not happen overnight.

In this book, will discuss the tactics abusers use to manipulate, deceive and control their victims, covertly and overtly for their gain. It's the journey to discover how deceivers manipulate their target underhandedly, behind the scenes, and with intention of their target being left in the dark. This book is not a healing journey to recovery, per say, but it opens the door to the dark, mischievous and underhanded methods emotional abusers use; it's the book they do not want written. In essence, once we expose the tactics, we can take the steps to heal on the journey, subsequently.

A manipulator wants to keep manipulating; this is the nature of the game. Once we see the hidden patterns, we are better suited to make empowered decisions. We will expose the tactics in broad daylight. This is the book I needed when I was learning about narcissistic abuse.

Family Life

I was the second child to my mother and father. I felt silenced, demeaned, put down, neglected, not heard, and came to the realization that I had to exit my family of origin from a young age. It was the most absurd thing to me – to know deep down my family was not for me. I had no idea why. They chose me to be brought into the world, so I was told, but by their actions, I was tolerated. I was not encouraged to be the best I could be, not supported with my ideas and was downtrodden for most of my upbringing.

If you were outside looking into to family, you perhaps, saw something different. My family kept up appearances. Large smiles and accolades when in public, but the private life did not compare. The shining beacon in my family was my grandmother, who was filled with joy and excitement at what was, just life. She was filled with love and attention and was truly sweet and genuine with a heart of gold.

I believe my sister was the golden child and I was the family scapegoat. This was the role I was to play, before I was even born – until I caught on!

Married

I got married for the first time at the ripe age of 40 to a man I met on an online dating website back in 2007. Not only was he good looking, tall at 6'2," but had a charismatic way about him. Too, not only was he witty, and smart, but he was different. Different, in the sense, that he didn't appear to be going through the motions.

I wanted to know him more. The more I came to know him, the more I wanted to know.

Through the next span of 8 years we kept in contact, and at times there were huge gaps in our relationship, so much so we would not speak for a year. When we reconnected, it felt as if time had no hold, and we picked back up where we left off. We started to seriously date in 2014, and eventually married in 2015, after about a year of dating exclusively. I remember succinctly when I decided in my heart that I loved him. I was all in. We wrote our own vows.

I felt like I knew him.

We divorced in 2016, after a year and a half of a devastating and unsettling marriage.

While this book is not a memoir, I mention my story a bit to let you, the reader, know I have been there. I have been through the pain of a devastating marriage, which, opened my eyes to the tactics emotional abusers use behind the scenes, to control, manipulate, and deceive, and then, in turn, use it against their victim to defame and silence.

This book is not to bash the narcissist or to seek revenge of any sort. It's to blow the lid off the covert abuse that occurs, detail the aspects of it, which is often not seen, and in most circles is not acceptable to talk about. This is to open the conversation, open the door in essence, to the abusive tactics, to educate on the schemes, so we are better positioned to make the best decisions.

It's empowerment. It's education. It's about validating your experiences so you can choose to rebuild, and from then, it opens the doors of things to come.

My hope is that you will be able to clearly see the schemes emotional/narcissistic abusers use, covertly and overtly, to recognize chronic behavior, so you can gain wisdom and understanding in what may be occurring in your relationship(s).

There may be many of you who may be faced with some decisions to make regarding your relationships. At the end of this book, I will provide some additional books and resources for guidance on this topic. There is also a list on our website, and new books are continually reviewed to be added.

I am proud of the many women (and men), who share their stories with bravery.

Writing Style

Many times, the pronoun, "She," will refer to the wife or the abused victim, whereas in referring to the abuser with using the "He," pronoun. Please feel free to swap the pronouns to suit.

The word narcissist at times may be interchanged with narcissistic abuser, narcissistic disordered individual, emotional abuser, toxic individual, manipulator and the like, or even partner/spouse where applicable.

At the same time, the word victim is used, but can be interchanged with target, survivor, or overcomer. There is a time, when a victim is a victim, but transforms into survivor.

My Story

For more information check out my website. I include a brief summary of my story there as well at:
https://www.movingforwardafterabuse.com/my-story/.

INTRODUCTION

This book is geared toward those who are in an emotionally devastating and manipulative relationship or marriage. It could be with your mother or father, partner, sister, brother, colleagues or boss.

This book may be hard to read, and I understand that.

The book is not written to shock and surprise, but the end results may be life-altering and you may end up rethinking your marriage or relationships.

The book may also cause some discomfort as we begin to explore the tactics abusers use. There is hope that goes beyond the standard "no contact" with the abuser.

Is this You?

- Do you find yourself in circular conversations that do not end, that only get worse?
- Do you find you feel you need to walk on eggshells in your relationship?
- Do you fear retaliation if you speak up and share your opinion?
- Do you have the feeling you don't know what's going on and are searching for answers?
- Is your brain searching for answers to confusing conversations, hours and days after they occurred, are you unable to make sense of the erratic conversations?
- After conversation with loved ones, do you find you cannot move an arm or even half of your body, feel in shock as to what just happened?
- Do you feel controlled, even manipulated and told what to say, how to act?

- Do you feel that you are doing everything you can to be perfect, run the house like a CEO, with no room for errors?
- Is something just not right and you are having a hard time trying to figure out what happened?
- Do you feel placated into believing that everything is your fault and that if you tried harder, things would be better?
- Do you feel unable to share your situation with others, especially those in your inner circle for fear of judgement, gossip, lack of understanding, and false accusations?
- Do you feel isolated, alone with no one to talk to or confide in?
- Are you constantly corrected, criticized and its wearing on you – how did things end up like this?
- Do you feel like you are sinking into nothingness? Do you feel as if your personality, joy, character traits and thoughts are disappearing?
- Have you felt at the absolute rock bottom in relationships and have felt there is absolutely no one you can turn to that would fully understand your situation or that no one would believe your side of the story?
- Do you feel like you are being emotionally robbed, powerless and your confidence is out the window?

If this is you, perhaps you feel like you are going crazy in your relationship. Perhaps you are exhausted from trying to perform and keep up with the demands put upon you.

The hope is that as we can uncover the hidden schemes, and see it in broad daylight, in a clear and organized fashion, you can make the best decisions possible for your situation.

If you are in a domestic violent situation, please contact your local authorities and/or please reach out the National Domestic Hotline.

National Domestic Violence Hotline 1-800-799-7233 (English)/1-800-797-3224 (En Español)

This book is a guidebook, that many do not want written, hopefully this will provide assistance, encouragement, and hope. We are going to begin with an overview on Narcissistic Personality Disorder.

OVERVIEW ON NARCISSISTIC PERSONALITY DISORDER

According to the Diagnostic Statistical Manual of Mental Disorders, or commonly known as the DSM, as of 2017, it is estimated that 6 percent of the U.S. population has Narcissistic Personality Disorder, or abbreviated as NPD. (Bree Bonchay, 2017). The DSM is the "go to" standard diagnostic guidebook, for industry mental health professionals.

Six percent of the U.S. population has Narcissistic Personality Disorder.

Let's calculate this information.

As of early 2020, the U.S. population has over 331 million people (Poston, 2020). Six percent of 331 million, is over 19 million people (19,860,000). According to this information, this means there are over 19 million people in the U.S. who have Narcissistic Personality Disorder, currently.

Let's do the math.

$$331,000,000 \times 6\% = 19,860,000 \text{ People}$$

19,860,000 people in the U.S. with Narcissistic Personality Disorder

It's likely you've been in contact with someone who has Narcissistic Personality Disorder.

This means, according to the DSM, there are over 19 million people who show the characteristic traits of: lack of empathy, grandiosity, and need for constant admiration.

Let's take it a little further.

If the average individual with Narcissistic Personality Disorder, abuses 4 people in their general circle, they can impact approximately 79 million people. Again, we are looking at just the U.S. figures.

$$19,860,000 \times 4 = 79,440,000 \text{ People}$$

79,440,000 people impacted by NPD in the U.S.

This is over 79 million people, who are potentially impacted by someone who has NPD.

Let's expand these figures globally.

According to the Worldometer, the world population, at the time of this writing, is over 7.8 billion people (Current World Population, 2020). Six percent of 7.8 billion people is 468,000,000. This means there is over 468 million people with Narcissistic Personality Disorder, *globally.*

$$7,800,000,000 \times 6\% = 468,000,000 \text{ People}$$

468,000,000 with Narcissistic Personality Disorder Worldwide

If these individuals abuse 5 people in their circle, they are impacting over 2.3 billion people worldwide (Bree Bonchay, 2017).

$$468,000,000 \times 5 = 2,340,000,000 \text{ People}$$

2,340,000,000 people impacted worldwide by NPD globally

It's hard to fathom these numbers, since they are so large. Just think about these numbers for a moment. A lot of people either have NPD, and/or are currently being impacted by it.

In addition, there are two additional layers that may catapult these figures in an upward trend. First, it is not common for someone with NPD to seek out therapy. Typically, if someone truly has NPD, a therapist is the last person they want to see. A narcissist is not one who wants to dive introspectively into their own behavior. They live in a notion they are entitled, are fully into self, and lack empathy.

Second, there is a lack of trained psychotherapists who can make an assessment to determine NPD. Many psychotherapists attended an institution which provided training and education for the role of a general psychotherapist. Narcissistic Personality Disorder, is a concentrated specialty, requiring more education and training, which many psychotherapists do not continue to achieve the level of skill required. Even if someone with NPD went to therapy, they may not be seeing the proper type of therapist, one who specializes in Narcissistic Personality Disorder, and therefore will not receive the proper diagnosis (Greenberg, 2019).

Given these additional layers, the numbers may be actually higher. There may be many individuals that exhibit traits, yet are not diagnosed, or who may never be diagnosed. The numbers may be exponentially higher, but it's a true unknown.

With the prevalence of Narcissistic Personality Disorder in society, it's likely there is someone in your circle, who has NPD, even if not diagnosed, and you have been impacted by it. It's imperative we learn about the disorder, so we can be adept in discerning (not diagnosing) the behavior for our situation.

Note: The author does not make any claims in diagnosing Narcissistic Personality Disorder or NPD, as this is reserved for qualified individuals, however, we will discuss this disorder from a broad based, birds-eye perspective, based on the research compiled, and validated by personal experiences.

Personality Disorders are grouped together by similarities in nature. Next, we are going to dive in to how personality disorders are organized by professionals into groupings, called clusters.

The Three Clusters of Personality Disorders

There are ten personality disorders grouped together by professionals into clusters. The clusters are Cluster A, B, and C, and are characterized by similarities in nature via the grouping. The traits each personality exhibits, is consistent, and is not based on chemical influences, is pathological, and the traits exist over a period of time in different situations. (Florida Behavioral Health, 2020).

Cluster A: Odd and Eccentric Personality Disorders (3)

- Schizoid Personality Disorder
- Schizotypal Personality Disorder
- Paranoid Personality Disorder

Cluster B: Dramatic and Erratic Personality Disorders (4)

- Histrionic Personality Disorder
- Borderline Personality Disorder
- Narcissistic Personality Disorder
- Antisocial Personality Disorder

Cluster C: Fearful and Anxious Personality Disorders (3)

- Obsessive-compulsive
- Dependent
- Avoidant

Narcissistic Personality Disorder ("NPD") is part of the broad spectrum of recognized Cluster B Personality Disorders, which includes Antisocial, Borderline and Histrionic. These personality disorders are grouped together since they show similarities in nature. The similarities are characterized by dramatic, overly emotional, or unpredictable thinking or behavior in interactions with others chronically (Cluster B personality disorders 2020). In this book, we are only going to discuss Narcissistic Personality Disorder.

Traits of Narcissistic Abusers

An individual with Narcissistic Personality Disorder, will use highly skilled manipulation tactics to deliberately isolate, deceive and control victims for their own personal gain of narcissistic supply.

Narcissists are a bully with a large case of egregious selfishness and entitlement but done with such charisma, intelligence, forethought and charm that oftentimes their deception goes unnoticed to the naked untrained eye. Narcissists wear a false mask and are masters of their trade. They emotionally abuse, take advantage of others, disregard boundaries, and lack true empathy.

In addition, these narcissistic disordered individuals are overly absorbed into "self" and are unaware of how their actions affect others. Narcissists have a constant need for attention whether positive or negative (supply), have a quick and over the top reaction to any perceived criticism, carry a victim-mentality, and avoid personal responsibility (BPD Central 2017).

At introduction with a narcissist, it can be very hard to detect someone who has Narcissistic Personality Disorder. Narcissistic abusers come across as charming, witty, charismatic and liked by many, yet when their "true self" is revealed, and their mask slips, we are in the beginning stages of seeing who they really are.

Now, it's worthy to note, that many people can exhibit signs of narcissism. It does not mean they have Narcissistic Personality Disorder. When someone has NPD, the traits are pathological, and continuous, not a one-time event. It's over and over again, chronic, and repeated.

There are many analogies that connect the personality of a narcissist, to that of the Dr. Jekyll/Mr. Hyde character. Let's look at it a bit further.

Dr. Jekyll/Mr. Hyde Character

Narcissists can be characterized by appearing at home one way, while another in public. This often is described as the Dr. Jekyll/ Mr. Hyde type personality. The character is one way in their outward life, which is often the charismatic, jovial side, so through outward appearances it will reflect how "good" they are. They may engage in charity functions, and be quick to help others in need while using language that displays true genuine care and concern, but are a different character in private than in public, which is their true self.

Please note the term character. The narcissist is just that, a character, an actor on display. The narcissist performs with certain traits in one environment for show, and they are incongruent in a separate environment.

The term, Dr. Jekyll and Mr. Hyde, stems from an 1886 book, written by Robert Louis Stevenson, which has been adapted into several movies and stage performances. Dr. Jekyll, a mind-mannered, controlled business man becomes Mr. Hyde, a sub-set of his character, and is transformed into an atrocious hideous character, after digesting a poisonous chemical. When the chemical wears off, the character is reverted back to his old self, Dr. Jekyll, with no memory of the transfiguration (Dr. Jekyll and Mr. Hyde character, 2020).

If you have grown up watching Bugs Bunny, you may remember the cartoon where Bugs Bunny is depicted against a "Hyde" character. It was released by Warner Bros. Looney Tunes in 1955 and is called Hyde and Hare (Freleng, 2018).

Perhaps you have been around a Dr. Jekyll/ Mr. Hyde character, and have been confused by the behavior. Maybe you are living with the character, or there is someone in your family that resembles some of the characteristics. You are not alone. With over 468 million people with

NPD globally and growing, many are impacted in the wake of the storm, by the tactics they use (which we get into in a later chapter).

Master Manipulators

Narcissists are master manipulators. If they were to show their true colors and intentions in the beginning of a relationship, there wouldn't be any takers. Who would voluntarily sign up to be with a controlling, ego-hungry emotional manipulator? No one would.

They cleverly orchestrate a certain persona to bring you into the relationship by using tactics. They do not reveal who they are, and once in a relationship with a narcissist, the mask starts to crack, and traits and characteristics of an abusive and toxic individual show. These traits may not show up for years or even decades later, as sometimes the face mask has been glued on.

What is important to mention here is that if you see pattern depicted with someone in your life, it's not necessary for them to have a formal diagnosis of a personality disorder. If there is a pattern of behavior that continues, over and over again, that shows signs of the tactics narcissists use on a repeated basis, then it's wise to believe you are in a toxic relationship (Saeed, 2020).

With so many people with Narcissistic Personality Disorder, you may wonder if there is a cure to date. Let's review.

Can Narcissistic Personality Disorder be Cured?

As of the writing of this book, according to broad based research and documentation in psychology, there is not a cure for Narcissistic Personality Disorder (Brazier & Klein, 2020).

Narcissistically disorder individuals oftentimes are unable to see themselves in proper light of their actions. They fail to evaluate personal actions to make changes that would be suitable. Oftentimes, the narcissist is not willing or able to do the emotional deep intensive internal heart change to uproot their personal beliefs and make a lasting change.

Will they fake change? Absolutely.

Will they claim they will do the work if called out on it? Yes, most of the time, these are fake promises. A narcissist will state they will change, but the words are empty as they fail to perform in action and accountability. They want to keep the abuse cycle intact (we will go into this in later); they don't want to change, and will placate *others into believing they will do the work* after exercising their other defense mechanisms.

The narcissist does not believe they can live their life any other way, nor do they want to. They are on the constant search for supply to uplift and support their frail ego. They cannot derive the supply they crave by their own merit. There is no personal accountability. Too, they have built up a defense mechanism so high that they will twist and turn the accusations toward another person or problem.

Everything is a game. It's a flip-the-switch-game of avoidance of personal responsibility of their actions. This flipping of the script, keeps them in a bondage to their own. If they cannot see the impact of their actions on others and they choose to live without taking responsibility of their behavior and it has been working for them (i.e., they are able to receive supply), then they have little to no reason to change.

What is important to note is people have to want to change for themselves. You cannot force an individual to be emotionally healthy. You cannot force someone to do anything. It has to be derived from their own choice and action.

People have to want to change. It's a personal decision. The narcissist fails in this aspect, as they fail to self-evaluate enough to make a change. The end result, is the narcissist stays the same, or gets worse as they age.

They deploy their other defense mechanisms into high gear, so they can be perpetually stagnant. They don't want to change. It's been working for them. They fail to see their impact and devastation on others. They lack the empathy. It's devastating to the victims in their path.

Many narcissists do not seek out counseling or get officially diagnosed.

People can change; however, this Cluster B Personality type has no documented evidence of anyone being cured to date.

Brain Scans Show Lack of Empathy in Narcissistic Personality Disordered Individuals

A study paper, published by Neuron in 2017, called *Empathic Care and Distress: Predictive Brain Markets and Dissociable Brain Systems*, report on the conclusion of MRI scans from 34 individuals, 17 of which who suffer from Narcissistic Personality Disorder. Researchers discovered that there is a distinction in the amount of gray matter between individuals with Narcissistic Personality Disorder and those who do not have NPD. What the study was able to conclude is that pathological narcissists had less gray matter in part of the cerebral cortex called the left anterior insula (Ashar et al., 2017).

The left anterior insula is connected to compassion and empathy. The link to the study has been placed in the resources, please take the time to review the study at your convenience. The study is continuing to evolve as scientists are learning more about the brain, and the link to empathy and the composition of the gray matter.

This is an amazing discovery! The narcissist wants you to believe that it's in your head. What is uncanny with this evidence, is the evidence is literally in the head of the narcissist, or lack thereof. This shows that narcissistic abuse is real, it's not a made-up fallacy, and it impacts the lives that come in contact with these disordered individuals. The science speaks for itself.

In order to understand Narcissistic Personality Disorder beyond traits and characteristics, we are going to look at what a narcissist needs, which triggers their actions, and is why they behave, as they do.

UNDERSTANDING NARCISSITS' BEHAVIOR

A narcissist needs constant supply. Supply is a fancy word which means attention drawn unto themselves. This attention or supply, can be in any form, good attention, or bad attention. They need this supply on a constant basis, and this forms the basic ground work in which they operate.

A narcissist may have a main source of supply, which could be a spouse or relationship partner; however, they typically have several sources of supply. If their main source is unavailable, they have multiple streams as a reserve, so they can be fed with a constant source of narcissistic supply. When a narcissist is able to obtain supply from a source, it keeps them going, and supplies them with a feeling of self-worth and importance. A narcissist generates the supply they need through tactics.

A narcissist will set the stage for a relationship to operate in a particular way from the beginning. This is where their acting skills come into play. A narcissist has six needs in any relationship, which sets the pace for this constant stream of supply.

Undying Devotion and Trust

A narcissist is searching for your undying devotion and trust. They accomplish this typically by sharing stories from their past, whether it be a past relationship, or a situation(s) they were part of, appearing to be a victim. They will show their "vulnerable side," setting the stage for you to have pity, empathy, and even admiration in exchange for your relentless allegiance. They need you to be on their side.

The narcissist begins to manipulate their target from the very first encounter. Time is not wasted, nor their carefully crafted words. They build their case from the start to draw you in. Their coercive nature may be entirely undetected at first, but it will increase. Eventually as time goes on, they will subtly require more of your attention to keep up with the demand.

Now, the stories the narcissist tells you from the start, may not be entirely true. They are told with the purpose of observing your reaction. They may be partially true, but with their own spin on the situation. It's a little bit twisted, to suit their outcome.

What is interesting to note right here, is the backward method a narcissist operates. They seek trust and devotion. In order for them obtain it, they require you, their target, to act trustworthy in increasing levels. They *act* trustworthy, but what they are doing is studying your response to their story.

The relationship is not built on true objectives of both parties establishing trust. The narcissist has a hidden agenda and they are looking for "buy-in" to their version of the story. They are looking for your reaction and they are recording your response. It's creepy, but they are studying you. Do you show pity? Are you empathetic? Are you trustworthy? If you are, this feeds the narcissist with supply and they will look to you as a continual source of supply should you keep providing.

When you provide a narcissist with the abilities of being trusted and can be devoted in a romantic relationship, they view you as a potential source of ongoing supply. Ultimately, the task, should you be able to get high marks in other categories, is for you to keep giving more, and more. They will want more and more supply, unending supply, in fact. Their demands will increase with you barely noticing, at first.

As a dominant priority, they are seeking to come first, and for you to put your other tasks on hold to suit their needs immediately; to the eventual cost of your personal goals and aspirations. They want allegiance. Sounds a bit over the top, no?

When in a relationship with a narcissist, they are takers, and are always asking for more. They need the reassurance to know you are a reliable source of supply for them. They need your unwavering devotion. This devotion feeds the narcissist with a constant source of supply.

In a healthy relationship there is devotion, and trust, etc. but it's a whole different game with a narcissist. The narcissist does not have pure motives that stem from a healthy relationship. They only want the devotion to suit them, as it's one-sided.

They are not looking to reciprocate this devotion back to you and, what makes it so confusing is they vocalize the right things. They will say lovely things at first, but their actions are not at all congruent. They speak vulnerably, but its false, so no vulnerability has really taken place.

Next, a narcissist is seeking your constant affirmation and admiration.

Note: While we may discuss being in a relationship with a narcissist in a partner relationship, please adapt these characteristics and traits to be for other members to include family and friendships.

Constant Admiration

Once a narcissist believes you trust them (or is it really them trusting you?), they will level it up by seeking continual admiration, attention, and approval. A narcissist needs to be cherished, honored, respected as the ultimate authority and "know-all" in your life.

They need your commitment, backing, devotion, and true belief in them to whatever they do. It's the buy-in.

In a healthy relationship, it's okay to admire your partner, and of course provide attention and support. What differentiates it is the constant request and goes beyond the boundaries of a healthy relationship. It's not healthy to have one partner who needs constant reassurance and admiration.

Power and Control

A narcissist needs to overpower you, wear you down to decrease your strength emotionally, physically, relationally, spiritually, financially – all of it, different angles at the same time, so that you will need them more and more. Overpowering you, fuels their feelings of grandiosity. They feel powerful and in charge. It supports their ego and entitlement. When there is one party who is dominant and overbearing, there is an unhealthy balance of power in the relationship. This dominance is maintained by one party controlling the other through manipulation tactics.

In a healthy relationship, partners build each other up, support, encourage and there is a proper balance of power in the relationship. One party may be "in charge" for a time, then the other party is. One party doesn't "lord it over" the other party on a consistent basis. There is sharing, personal responsibility, contribution for the health and longevity of the relationship. Both parties are focused on each other's needs, wants, and are reciprocal with shared empathy.

Value and Importance

A narcissist is looking to have merit, value, and be adept; however, what sets them apart from a healthy individual is the skill at which they try to prove their value. Oftentimes, a narcissist will exaggerate in order to show their expertise. Exaggerating helps them to hide their fragile self-esteem (Ni, 2018).

Reaction

After a narcissist emotionally abuses or take advantage of you in some way, a narcissist is looking for your strong reaction to their abuse. They receive glory from it on the inside and relish that they have been powerful enough to cause you distress. This is narcissistic supply. It feeds them. At the same time, when you do react, they will use it against you, which may cause yet another reaction from you, and this continues. The cycle of abuse will detail this aspect further.

Silence

Once the narcissist knows you are devoted to them, their requirements get deeper. After showing the narcissist you can be trusted, and can provide them with ample supply on- the-regular, they need your complicit silence in response to their actions.

A narcissist will do something out of the ordinary, something just not quite right, and will test you to see how you behave. It may start out as something small at first.

Do you keep silent?

A lot of times, a narcissist will use fear or intimidation tactics to keep you silent so you will not speak up at an injustice. They may threaten. They may raise their voice. They need your trained obedience to keep silent. They need to know you will fuel them with supply, no matter how obtuse their behavior gets. They are testing you.

At this point in the relationship with the narcissist, you may struggle with keeping your own independence, your own thoughts, opinions, as the viewpoints of the narcissist are meshing in and you are taking on the persona that they are creating you to be.

What is interesting, is that there are levels of devotion to the narcissist. At first, they would not ask your silence to their obtuse behavior, as the level of commitment and devotion was not there. Too, they needed to be able to control, and manipulate you by using their skilled tactics, which takes a little bit of time for their victims to be conditioned into the behavior they seek.

The narcissist wants you to remain silent after emotionally disturbing events. Not only do they not want to be accountable for their behavior, but by you remaining silent, they can continue their obtuse behavior and are receiving the supply.

When a narcissist has these six needs met, it sets the foundation for a predictable cycle of abuse.

THE ABUSE CYCLE

A narcissists' behavior is predictable in that it follows a repeated pattern of abuse. There are three stages that make up the abuse cycle: Love-Bomb, Devalue and Discard.

Narcissists will begin a new relationship by showering with attention, over-the-top compliments, and will appear to be overly attentive in the Love-Bomb Stage. In the Devalue Stage, they will mock, belittle, and exacerbate their victim in some fashion. Then lastly in the Discard Stage they may either leave the relationship altogether, move on to other areas of supply, and/or be completely disinterested and unengaged in the current relationship. If they wish to re-engage due to being low on supply, they will go to Stage 1 and Love-Bomb their victim to draw them back in. Put this on repeat.

This very cycle can go on for years, over and over again with variances, but the stages are the same. The cycle of abuse, like other tactics the narcissists use, are not easily detectable, as they will mix up their style to avoid accountability and exposure.

Too, if they believe their target is catching on their schemes, the level and intensity of deception increases. The narcissist is a skilled master manipulator orchestrating the drama in perfect harmony as their victim stands unaware.

The First Stage – Love-Bombing

The narcissist is an actor. They will act a certain way to get what they want.

The term *love-bombing* was derived from a leader of a church with a cult-like following, Sun Myung Moon in the 1970's. The congregants were over the top complementarians to other members and visitors of the church. The term also has been used by gang leaders to generate control and loyalty from pimps (MacMillan, 2018).

Love-Bombing is not a new concept. Even though the term, love-bombing, was coined in the 1970's, the roots can be traced back to the beginning of time.

Love-Bombing is engaging in false flattery, high-level or over-the-top compliments for a certain gain.

The narcissist becomes an actor, falsely praising his victims in order to achieve his objectives, which is for narcissistic supply. The narcissists plan is to hook and control victims for their own gain. Love-bombing is one method and is typically a tactic used in the beginning of a relationship and then part of the abuse cycle.

A narcissist will be kind, display his false self, be courteous, thoughtful, warm, and sensitive to woo the victim.

The words hold no merit. Their acting skills are in full force showcasing their best skills and assets. It's all a front, and is the start of the cycle.

In the Beginning of a New Relationship:

In the beginning of a relationship, love-bombing can sound like:

- "Your eyes are so beautiful; they light up the sky…"
- "I have never seen someone as (smart, sexy, witty) as you…"
- "I believe we are meant to be together…"

Or:

- Constant delivery of flowers with special notes
- An offer to take a vacation to a special elaborate place in the beginning of the relationship, NYC, Bali, Hawaii, France, sailing in the Caribbean two weeks in to the relationship;
- Off the top, romantic gestures;
- Sending elaborate gifts early on in the relationship to your work office; and/or

- Excessive text messages, showering affection, love to a high extent, and over the top (White, 2018).

While these statements and gestures sound endearing, they are not. They are above normal compliments. The narcissist is trying to win you over, and to do so quickly. They are on a mission. They seek to progress the relationship forward rapidly, and this is their method. Love-Bombing is over-the-top. It's flattery to the highest extent.

Many people love to be complimented. The narcissist finds special qualities and largely compliments them in abundance, which draws in their victim. The victim loves the attention, and believes this sets the tone of the relationship, and they look forward to being on the receiving end of this magical development and continues on in the relationship. The narcissist has hooked their target.

In the Middle of the Relationship

In the middle of a relationship, the narcissist, will revert back to this stage after they have devalued and discarded. The narcissist will love-bomb if they need to "reel in" their target on subsequent go rounds, love-bombing sounds a bit different here, for example, it can sound like:

- "I love you so much; I would never do anything to hurt you…"
- "You know I would never do anything like that to you…."

Or:

- "I cherish the ground you walk on…"
- You are my everything…"

The narcissist has the gall to make these bold statements and many victims believe it, for years, since it sounds so good and many want to believe it, and do for a while. What has occurred is the victims have been conditioned to believe the narcissist, over their own intuition. The victim truly believes the narcissist won't hurt them, because they say so, until the light bulb moment occurs, and they can see the false claims the narcissist makes repeatedly.

Love-Bombing will also include false promises (things they state that sound like such a good idea, but they have no intention of following through with it) such as:

- Next weekend, why don't we spend some time together, just you and I to do…
- They will show tender affection and gentleness and say something like, "now, this is the type of relationship, I want to have…"

These false promises are just that words to get you to come back. They are positive, fulfilling, even fun. The narcissist has studied you from the beginning of the relationship, and knows what you would like to see, so they promise it. They say, I will do X, and whatever X is, they say they will do it, but when the time comes for it to be done, either they:

- Claim they forgotten about it
- State they never said they would do it
- Pick a deliberate fight before a special event
- Say they will be out of town
- Make up an excuse on why they cannot do it
- Change the relationship status (breaking up), etc. so they don't have to do what they "claimed" they said they would do.

There is really no limit to the false claims they state.

If you buy into their claim, they will continue with their same behavior.

Love-Bombing Toward the End of a Relationship

If the narcissist believes you are on to their tactics of love-bombing, they will still love-bomb, though it will uniquely different. They will go back to appearing vulnerable and even lost saying:

- "You are my all in all, I only want to be with you…"

One of the biggest fears for a narcissist is abandonment, so they may say:

- "When you left, I felt abandoned…"

They want to bring you back.

The targeted individual in relationship with a narcissist, oftentimes is empathic. An empath is one who can see and feel the emotions of others. The last thing an empath wants to do is to cause someone else to feel abandoned, by their actions. Many empaths may choose to stay in the relationship at this point, so the narcissist is not abandoned.

The narcissist wins, and have been successful in bringing you back. The cycle of abuse can continue.

Love-bombing sounds different in the various stages of a relationship. Overall, what characterizes it is the over-the-top words, and is based in flattery.

Next, is the Devaluing Stage.

The Second Stage-Devalue

After the narcissist has been successful in winning you over in the love-bombing stage, the next pattern of abuse is to Devalue.

When a narcissist begins the Devalue stage, they are going to attack something you do or say, or just something about you, which may cause offense. They may devalue you directly with high level of criticism (though it starts of small and escalates), or will belittle, ignore, or discredit you.

The ultimate goal is to wear you down, emotionally, even physically. They have a whole host of tactics to devalue their victim. Devaluing is the opposite of everything supportive in a true healthy relationship with genuine love, care and concern.

Devaluing is to knock you down a notch, to reduce your self-esteem, self-worth, and with the long-term goal of reducing your ability or even desire to exit the relationship. In this stage, trauma is introduced, as the narcissist is prone to obtuse abusive behavior, as the narcissist exhibit all sorts of tactics on you to have you think less of yourself.

As a response to the behavior, you may turn on yourself, and work to correct the issue. If the narcissist has attacked you clothing or hair style, you will work harder to look prettier, or have a better haircut. If your cooking skills were attacked, you will try to make better meals. If the narcissist has attacked your car, or job, friends, you will work on these items to improve in order to bring the relationship back where it was in the love-bombing stage, where the narcissist was highly complementary.

Notice the turning on self: A narcissist conditions their victims (groomed) to not respond with self-respecting behavior, such as standing ground, standing up for yourself, calling out things that are not right, etc. The victim is being worn down and deliberately. The victim, takes on the responsibility of the infraction, because they want the relationship to revert back to the love-bomb stage. Too, they choose to not stand up for themselves, because, there may be consequence if they do…

Devaluing is a confusing stage. Just before this stage, you were in the love-bombing stage, and perhaps thought the relationship was wonderful, as it was in a glory stage. Then, the narcissist has a quick turn of behavior and they are highly critical and often, curt, short, unloving, and appear to be a different person (Dr. Jekyll/Mr. Hyde).

The Devalue Stage is a complete shift from the previous. The narcissist, is no longer showering you with over-the-top compliments, but they are administering the opposite, bringing you down in any way. The very things they may have complimented weeks, days, or hours earlier, are now being attacked. The narcissist wants you to think less of yourself, suffer the emotional harm, back down, and to make matters even more interesting, to take it in silent submission. Before they said they wanted to take a trip with you, now they say you are the worst traveling companion.

The narcissist sets you up to believe, that if you fix whatever they insult, the relationship will go back to the love-bombing stage. The love-bomb is their backup. If they could win you over with it in the beginning of the relationship, and you bought it, they know they can lure you back holding this ideology over your head. They are teasing you with holding the carrot. If only you would do XYZ, then the relationship would go back to normal. It's all part of this cycle, round and round it goes.

Too, what is also going on in the background as the narcissist devalues, is they are urging you to have a large reaction to their behavior. They will keep pushing your buttons with increasing intensity. They want you to have an angry outburst, and the moment you do, it will be used against you.

Some narcissists may even laugh when you have had an angry outburst. The narcissist is laughing simply because they are rejoicing that they have pushed you to your limits and they have a reaction from you – which is fuel for their narcissistic supply.

They will keep criticizing, and putting you down devaluing, in any way they can. It may be constant, and you may feel the narcissist is picking on your every move. They are. They are doing it deliberately.

They devalue you for a reaction, positive or negative. They enjoy your reaction. If you are hurt, they receive supply. If you are upset and confused with their devaluation, they are encouraged to continue to do more since it's the reaction they are seeking and needing.

Devaluing is so painful and so detrimental because it robs us from everything we were meant to be. It gets us to our core. It hits home and so deeply. It attacks our character. It reduces us. We feel small and insignificant. Our identity is impaired and fractured and our self-esteem takes a punch in the gut, especially as the abuse endures for years.

The Third Stage – The Discard

The third stage in the abuse cycle, is the Discard stage. The narcissist, has another source of supply and no longer needs the relationship in the same capacity.

This is the stage where the narcissist has moved on. They have sought out a new reliable source of supply and the relationship is not what is used to be and/or the narcissist is completely disengaged in the current relationship.

The relationship can end abruptly, oftentimes with you wondering what happened and why all of a sudden.

The narcissist has discarded their victim since they believe this source of supply has either caught on to their manipulations, have other source(s) lined up, and/or if they are just not getting the reactions from the current relationship as they need. They need greater supply and they have been searching for it. When they have found it, they move on and you are discarded. They move on to the next victim and love-bomb them to start the cycle over.

Additional Stages

Self-proclaimed narcissist, HG Tudor, provides additional stages and are:

- Stale Stage
- Disobedience Stage
- See Through Stage
- Hoover Opportunity Stage
- Total Control Stage

The Stale Stage

In the beginning of a new relationship with their anticipated target, according to Tudor, the narcissist is delighted with the level of fuel. As a new relationship is formed, there is a high level of interaction, and this is awesome fuel for the narcissist.

When the relationship progresses and is established to on a more "comfortable level", the level of fuel decreases for the narcissist, and the relationship enters a "stable," yet perceived as stale, level. This stale level does not carry the new excitement from the beginning of the relationship, and this is viewed as a decrease in fuel. This decrease is the relationship weakness, according to Tudor. The narcissist fears the relationship will not continue with the same level of fuel as from the beginning, and it causes the narcissist to take action that will increase the level of fuel delivered to them.

The Disobedience Stage

The narcissist believes the sole purpose of the relationship is to receive supply. When there is lack, this is viewed as disobedience, and the narcissist increases their level of control. They move to the next step in the plan, in the words of Tudor, they narcissist moves from "dictator to malign tyrant."

See Through Stage

If the narcissist believes you are seeing red flags in the relationship, gaining wisdom and discernment about the behaviors you are seeing, have others in your life that speak truth and wisdom, the narcissist is now a nervous wreck. The narcissist does not want you to discern the red flags, which may open you up to learn more about their hidden agenda. They do not want to be found out; they cannot be found out. If they believe that you may have some inkling, that you are on to them, they must but a dire stop to it, and right away, and it will be a big commotion.

In this stage, they unleash cruel and intentional games to cause your mind to spin, to traumatize, and will deploy any tactic to do so. They have to keep you as source of fuel and better yet, keep you subjected to their rule and authority in your life. They remind you how they once thought you viewed them, with such honors, and they will call you out unexpectedly on how you have waned. This is their internal cry for supply.

They deploy the art of devaluing you. They will turn the tables so things are your fault and it is your responsibility to fix them. Their requests are outlandish and confusing and even if you comply, they are never enough. The carrot keeps moving. They want you to defend yourself, then, they will call you out on it. They are turning the tables to confuse and disorient you, so your footing is unstable and unclear. They cannot have their true self be exposed.

The narcissist will use your strengths against you, your empathy, compassion and willingness to work out issues in a relationship. They do this, so you will take a step back at whatever they feel was uncomfortable for them (not enough supply given to them), in order for you to step up your fuel supply for them.

This stage is designed so you, the target, are in a confused state, and unable to make sound decisions; your will is reduced and you freefall back into *their* purpose for you. They know it causes harm to you, but do not care. The purpose is for their supply. It protects their hidden agenda. They must never be called out on their behavior.

The Hoover Opportunity

The hoover opportunity does not occur with the current target, it happens when a previous source of supply, has re-emerged. The narcissist will explore this opportunity and test the waters to see if it will suffice for continued support. If, in favor for the narcissist, they have found another source of supply, they will begin to question why they sought you (their most recent target) for a relationship. If the previous source of supply, ends the supply connection, then the narcissist will treat his current ongoing supply with love bombing – and the cycle repeats.

Total Control

The narcissists objective is total control; everything from what you say and do, to what you are not doing. There is no end to the vast requirements of total control. It is all encompassing and whatever attempt the victim makes, will not be adequate.

The narcissist evaluates their ability to control based on the way victims respond during the time of intentional devaluation. If the narcissist believes to have full and total control, they are supplied. The target is judged by their response to the devaluation and is viewed as a reliable and dependable if they deliver. This then, becomes not adequate enough supply because it is no longer supreme compliance via the lens of the narcissist. The narcissist doesn't want just adequate supply, as they will always want more. When doing the very thing they want, the narcissist turns and continues to devalue (Tudor, 2020).

It's maddening.

There is no positive outcome of being in a relationship with a narcissist. The stages continue to cycle, the narcissist does not receive the supply they seek, their victim is left in a confusing state of affairs. These stages can come at any time, in any order and without notice. The mastery behind it is evil and destructive and the best way to handle is to go no contact, or grey rock, with the narcissist; however, going no contact, or grey rock, is just the beginning.

Next, there has been much discussion and a lot back and forth on addressing victims as codependent. We are going to compare Abused vs. Codependent in this setting.

Abused vs. Codependent

According to an article titled, "Codependent or Abused" (Ford-McComb & Hubacher, Family Crisis Shelter), the victim in the relationship, has *been trained to respond* by years of being the abuse cycle, and has determined the abused are not codependent. A codependent is one who is unable to master the skill of independence as suitable, and, in exchange, takes on responsibility for another. When there is a relationship with an emotional narcissistic abuser, the targets are abused. We are going to compare and contrast the two:

- **Codependent:** Carries the responsibility for feelings and behaviors of others;
- **Abused**: The emotional abuser holds *their victim* responsible for their feelings and behaviors.

As a trained response, the abused has to anticipate and read the face and body language in order to be prepared, as best as possible for the narcissists' erratic behavior. Many develop C-PTSD, and become hyper-vigilant as a response.

- **Codependent**: Has inability to express feelings. The codependent needs to be often validated and given permission to share by their other party.
- **Abused**: "If I share how I truly feel, my life could be at risk by my significant other."

The abused in this circumstance has learned "to stuff" feelings, for when shared prior, there was a penalty such as being mocked, humiliated, belittled, ignored or other.

- **Codependent**: Fear of being emotionally hurt and personally rejected. Validation to proceed before freedom to share is sought in the relationship.
- **Abused**: The abused has a learned physical and mental response to the emotional pain and neglect in her relationship.

The abused has been injured and yet, there may not be bruises on the body, the abused lives in a constant alert state. At the simplest gesture, there may be an instant where your spouse/partner has exploded in rage. By moving left, the victim could be berated, and to the right, verbal assault. Being in a relationship with a narcissist, it paralyzes emotionally and mentally with each repeated act of manipulation and control.

- **Codependen**t: "The words that I speak, I filter through the approval and perceived judgements of others. I do not believe I have merit or worth, and especially in vocalizing my opinions. I do not matter enough."
- **Abused**: "I am at risk for everything I say, or don't say, what I do, or don't do, my motives are questioned even if unspoken. I am in the corner of the wall and I cannot move. I am inept and worthless (Lambert, 2018)."

When emotional narcissistic abuse is happening the targeted victim slowly loses themselves. When in a controlling, abusive narcissistic environment, the target is victimized into being a prisoner and is traumatized over and over, and the sense of worth and value diminishes at an unprecedented pace, and as planned by her abuser (Ford-McComb & Hubacher, Family Crisis Shelter).

Many times, people are ostracized and oftentimes demeaned due to lack of understanding on why they stay in abusive relationships. Hopefully this information will assist to shed light on the risk levels for the abused and why it is difficult to exit the relationship. Furthermore, we are going to discuss the tactics narcissists use to gain supply.

33 TACTICS USED BY THE NARCISSIST

"If you tell a lie long enough, it becomes the truth." Joseph Goebbels

Narcissists are infamous for using tactics to get their target to act and think in a certain way. Their tactics are vast and are unseen especially in the beginning of a relationship. They hope they are never found out, while subtly increasing their level of control and manipulation. After time, their mask slips, and we can detect the chronic behaviors they do not want seen.

In this chapter, we are going to discuss 33 tactics narcissists commonly use, through this list is exhaustive, it may not list all the tactics. The purpose of itemizing these tactics is so we can detect and see the deception, clear as day.

Gaslighting

The term "gaslighting" stems back to a 1938 play, entitled Gas Light, which was later adapted in 1944 to Gaslight, a psychological-thriller film which was nominated for seven academy awards including best picture, Best Actor and Best Screenplay. In the film, the husband deliberately manipulates his wife to believing the house they share is haunted. He flickers lights, rearranges furniture, creates noise to cause her to go insane and to be distracted from his mischief.

Gaslighting is a control technique that narcissists use to usurp your reality. They are trying to re-frame events, facts, details, stories, in a way that suits their antics. They are re-conceptualizing what you should believe, based on their twisted rendition of the story.

They are trying to have you doubt yourself and recollection of events, details and facts. Gaslighting is crazy-making behavior. It causes disorientation and over time you lose yourself.

After being gaslight, the narcissist will have prepared responses to your questioning. They will claim your rendition of facts never happened, are delusional, or lying. They will state your memory is not right, that you are getting old, or have some disorder. They will lie and make up a contrary story. They want you believe what they tell you.

Not only does gaslighting cause self-doubt, but it provides for layered covert forms of abuse, simultaneously, for example dismissiveness. Not only will the narcissist dismiss your story, but they will interrupt, before you have time to explain your point of view. They say you are misinformed. They discredit and belittle. They call out a time when you were wrong about something, and say it's just like that situation. They want you to second-guess yourself and then ultimately believe in their twisted story. Narcissists will threaten. They will intimidate. They will make up things others have said and use it against you. They are convincing in the language and tone of voice used.

The narcissist's plan is to wear you down mentally. They want to destroy your intuition and your desire to speak up and contradict, when something is not right.

A narcissist may even laugh at you, when they are gaslighting you, partially because they know it's a game, they have mastered the skills of deception, and they take pleasure in this game. This is, of course, until we wake up and see the destructive behavior.

Once the narcissist observes their target is connecting the dots of mischief, they will either amp up their manipulation or devalue so horrifically, that the focus has then shifted; a major distraction. This distraction takes the focus off the gaslighting and devaluation, for a time, and adds fuel to the self-doubt and confusion.

Gaslighting is a deliberate distortion of reality to control another. The narcissist chooses to gaslight at a time when their victim believes them. They use the established trust against their victim. This creates self-doubt and is crazy making behavior. The victim starts to think they were wrong, believe they didn't see the situation clearly, and after being worn down emotionally for a while, they give up and just trust the narcissist's perception on reality.

Cognitive Dissonance

Gaslighting leads to cognitive dissonance. Cognitive dissonance is when the brain is conflicted based on incongruencies between what someone says and does; it is observing hypocrisy at its finest. The inconsistent behavior causes mental confusion. The mind circulates to try to make sense of the contrast in the behavior observed, and words spoken (Legg & Leonard, 2019).

The narcissist, has no intention in living a congruent life, and to do what they say. The words spoken are only to dissuade, and are for show. The narcissist has no desire to do what they claim. The game is to see how long they can continue, undetected. Here are some examples of cognitive dissonance in a partner relationship:

- Being physically abused while the abuser says it's for your own good, and they had to do it.
- They claim they will be there for you, but repeatedly fail to hold up their side of the bargain.
- The narcissist states, "I would never do anything to hurt you..." (but emotionally or physically damages consistently.)
- The narcissist says they love you, but show no signs of it, and the evidence is lacking, repeatedly.

For a time, the victim believes the narcissist. They have bought the words. They believe in what they are told.

After time, the victim begins to see to see incongruencies in behavior. They can see the manipulation, mere words with no backing behind it, and this is the start of the mental shift that occurs.

Even after receiving clarity in the situation, there is a still a struggle to see the narcissist for who they are, and this is what keeps many stuck in a cognitive dissonance state.

Cognitive dissonance is the way the brain protects itself, to avoid the truth of the situation, for a time. It helps the brain to minimize the discrepancy and trauma from events. We want to believe in what the narcissist says, and want to believe they have our best interest in mind, but over time of repeated failed actions, we see their words do not add up. The truth is sometimes hard to hear. No one wants to believe their marriage or relationship is not based on a solid foundation of trust.

Not only is it imperative to see the cognitive dissonance displayed, but when we can accept it, can we make changes to move forward.

When the narcissist gaslights, this causes cognitive dissonance. The cognitive dissonance is one reason many victims, even after leaving the relationship, remain still impacted by the relationship and struggle with healing. As after they discern the relationship, many still find the abusive treatment they endured to be hard to swallow.

It does take time to heal this aspect of the relationship after exiting. The longer there is separation, it allows for deep level so emotional healing can occur.

Stockholm Syndrome

When in a relationship with a toxic, emotional abuser, oftentimes a "trauma bond" is formed between the abuser and their victim. The victim experiences trauma from being in the relationship, and feels connected to the abuser so much so, they turn on themself in light of protecting their abuser. The victim will side with their abuser to prevent further abuse and is form of survival, and results from cognitive dissonance.

The term, Stockholm Syndrome, comes from a 1973 bank heist in Stockholm, Sweden - a bank robbery, turned into a six-day heist where hostages developed a bond with their captor (Eschner, 2017). A movie, called Stockholm, released in 2018, played by Ethan Hawke, reenacts the heist.

Narcissists cleverly perform tactics, which cause their victim's emotional harm. Their motivation is not pure. It's important to take a closer look at additional tactics narcissists use.

Testing and Overriding Boundaries

If you have a boundary, you better believe the narcissist will test it and try to override it.

Narcissists will be subtle at first, but will target your boundary with increasing measure to wear you down. They may even cause a made-up crisis for you to override your boundary.

Narcissists do not like boundaries, therefore they are attracted to those who do not have firm boundaries, and who want to keep the peace.

Narcissists, do not like being told no, or they cannot do something, as they construe it as a challenge. Many believe, a narcissist is like a 5-year-old child. They want their way, they may cry, so you give in. A similar philosophy occurs with narcissists. A narcissist will test you to see how far you will stretch. They will start off slow and see if they can get you to change your priorities.

When a narcissist overrides a boundary, they are disrespecting you and, saying your personal limits do not matter. They feel entitled to over-step. By disrespecting you and your boundaries, they are sending a few signals that are noteworthy:

- Narcissists must control and dominate. When you set a boundary, you are setting a limit on what you find acceptable and not. Someone who respects you, will respect your boundaries.

- When a narcissist oversteps, they are saying they matter more, their needs are more important and what they say goes.
- When a narcissist overrides your boundaries, it has an impact on other areas not only the issue they chose to overstep. Once they can undermine your authority by overstepping a boundary, they will continue to overstep in other areas.

If you set a firm boundary with a narcissist, there will be hell to pay. The abuse will get worse, they may scream and yell, causing an absolute fit, like the 5-year-old. When they get their way, the feel empowered overpowering you, and it feeds their sense of self-worth and false ego.

When a narcissist overrides your boundaries, we may feel less than, not valued in the relationship, nor respected. Please note, this is deliberate. They want you to feel this way, which is their motivation.

Discrediting and Belittling

Discrediting is when a toxic individual puts you down, doesn't apply worth or value to your statement or opinion. They may cut you off even in mid-sentence, interrupt you as you are sharing your opinion and will speak to the contrary.

The emotional abuser, will belittle; call it a backhanded compliment (sounds good on the outside, but it's meant to hurt). It may sound like a compliment (and claim they are trying to bring levity into the conversation), but it's an underhanded slap in the face during serious conversations. Then, of course if you call them out, and say it offends you, they will say they were trying to bring some levity into the discussion. To you, this isn't the time for levity, some conversations require serious adult communication. This is a distraction. So, now may feel you need to teach how to carry on an adult conversation and when it's appropriate to have levity and when to be serious. Then, to add confusion, the narcissist, will throw out that you took it wrong, that you are too sensitive, and that you should go with the flow more, that you are getting old and have lost your sense of humor and can't' take a joke anymore and why are they even with you. Put this on repeat.

This is emotional abuse. Let's call this for what it is. This is not acceptable behavior.

The victim believes they must change and modify behavior at whatever caused the incident. The victim wants to do better. They try to fix themselves. They work on issues. They take upon themselves the responsibility of the unknown to fix what caused the incident. They work on trying to be more credible so they are not attacked.

This is crazy making behavior, to demean you, to cause you emotional harm and to undermine your position or authority.

While discrediting you, the toxic individual is building a holy army against you with weapons to weaken you one limb at a time, until your spirit waves the white flag either in submission to, in which case you will continue to be abused, or they will discard you entirely. Afterward, you are left to try to figure out and pick up the pieces; there is no win in this situation.

Belittling is a tactic that is used to try to make someone else feel inferior, small, and less important. It's literally to "be little." The narcissist will try to get you to feel less than, so they can feel big, important and empowered. It's a form of minimizing.

Have you heard:

- "She doesn't know what she is talking about!"
- "She's just a (fill in the blank), this could be anything."
- "You really believe that?"

Let's walk through a hypothetical example:

You share a dream with your spouse or partner, that you wish you accomplish "X." Of course, "X" requires you to obtain more skills, and you are up for the challenge. You are excited and look forward to learning new things, and see a ton of great rewards for both of you.

Partner replies, "Why don't you do something you are good at?"

In 9 short words, so many things are happening, and to many, it sounds positive, and even encouraging, but lets' break it down in a deceptive, toxic, and manipulative environment.

This is what is occurring:

- Partner is not encouraging you to pursue a passion.
- Partner is trying to prevent you from moving forward to learn new things.
- Partner fears your new skills may over shadow their need for supply. Your attention will be drawn away from them and into other things. Partner fears you may become successful. Then, they have to compete with you, which they cannot tolerate.
- Your desire to improve your skills, challenges partner's ego. Partner must be boss, superior, and you cannot be.
- Notice the way it's spoken; it sounds like it's a positive question. Yes, we should do things we are good at, but partner is trying to shut down your exploration of ambition. Its stated in such a way to cause self-doubt. You may think, yea, I should just put this new passion at bay, since there is so much to learn, why even start.
- Partner is trying to close your vision, and to shut the door of opportunity.
- Partner fears your ambitions will lead to other ventures, so it must be shut down from the onset. Partner does not want you to "get out of control" and therefore out of obedience to the mission they have chosen you for. You are not to have a separate life purpose. Your life purpose, according to this toxic partner, is to serve their mission, until they no longer need you. Partner is

condescending and patronizing. It is a put down-in disguise of them looking out for your best interest.

Learning new skills builds confidence and self-assurance among other positive mindsets. This will be taken as a threat and the turmoil will increase so as to cause you to not be able to pursue your new adventure. And, with all the new turmoil, it will become nearly impossible to move forward. You eventually give up the desire and remain in the emotional abuse.

Your partner spent 5 seconds in a response to your dream, and it has a torpedo-like-effect not only in the relationship, but your personal aspirations have been impacted. They want to dominate, control what you do, and it's only their way. There is no negotiating. There is no discussion. It is shot down.

Your spirit is crushed. Your hope diminished. You put your passion aside and believe they are right. They know best.

Have you seen this scenario play out in your relationship?

This is why a relationship with a narcissist is destroying your soul! They are crushing dreams, visions, purpose, and delight in your vision. They are against everything that breathes life into you. This is why it's imperative to no longer allow them to control, manipulate or perpetuate their abuse any longer.

Other Examples of Belittling Behavior:
- Being treated like a child.
- Undermining Behavior. They mock and make fun of you and say how cute is that you suggested something then laugh at it.
- They will call you out on what they deem to be your stupidity all with their innocence and fake humor.
- When you ask a question on something, they will use it against you and treat you like you were born yesterday and don't know anything.

In your mind, you honestly want to learn, but they will mock you, especially if you ask around others, and try to make you feel small and insignificant, repeatedly, and in many cases, this is from a loved partner.

A narcissist likes to add insult to injury. When you are already in a state of confusion stemming for a previous episode, and have not recovered, they like to add a salt to the wound, it can be one word, which add another brick to the previous injury. They want to keep their victim in a perpetual state of emotional agony, because then, its challenging to have a clear head. It keeps us hyper-vigilant and on the lookout for our next attack and mentally wears us out.

Reinforcement Re-Gaslight

Reinforcement gaslighting occurs when share our experience with others. Others may not understand the dynamic of narcissistic abuse and may also employ tactics to keep us in the abuse, without directly knowing what they are.

Relationships do call for compromise and adjusting to one another, but be aware that others may not understand and, may also discredit, minimize or even belittle what they perceive are your circumstances.

Isolation

A toxic individual will try to separate you from your trusted friendships and family. This process starts when the narcissist has the first encounter with your friends and family. They want your support network to dry up. If you have no support network, it increases the likelihood you will remain in the abusive environment.

The process of isolating you from your friends and family is not an overnight process, rather it happens gradually, but the narcissist is conditioning you (and them, unbeknownst to you) to respond in a certain way with mixed and confusing messages.

Let's take a look at an example scenario that can play out as the narcissist sets the stage from the beginning when meeting your extended network.

Example: Outside Network:

1. From the beginning, when your partner meets your friends and family for the first time, they have set themselves up with a positive image. They are friendly, charismatic, fun, and an all-around pleasure to be around. Your friends and family will have this image of your partner/spouse and will see them in a positive light.
2. Eventually as the relationship progresses, your partner will discredit you behind your back to your friends and family and will try to win your family and friends over by manipulation.
3. Your partner will reach out to your family, to try to build their case to side with them. The narcissist is seeking empathy and compassion, even pity from your support network, and to be positioned to take their side, should the relationship go sour at some point in the future. By doing this, they are causing your support network to fail, should they not see through the scheme.

The narcissist plants seeds from the beginning, for your friends and family to take their eyes off of them as a potential problem and to place it on you. When the relationship goes sour, your own support network may turn against you as you have been likely discredited behind your back.

The narcissist, realizes, once you catch on to their scheme, the relationship may go kaput. So, they plan in advance (years) so your friends and family will buy their story which leaves you in isolation.

This is devastating to the victim as when they leave the relationship, they come to realize their friends (and family) may have been manipulated and have turned against them. This is why leaving a narcissist is difficult and overwhelming. They, not only destroy the 1:1 relationship individually, but it has an impact on the extended network.

Many overcomers of narcissistic abuse, have to restart their whole lives over, new friends, as the narcissist has coerced years of friendships.

The Narcissist Fears your True Friends and Family

While the narcissist wants to isolate you from your friends and family, at the same time, they fear your engagement with your loved ones. Your true friends and family will look out for your best interest and will evaluate for red flags.   The narcissist fears this evaluation because:

- They do not want to be exposed. Friends and family may see red flags that you are unable see, and they may open your eyes to it.
- They cannot be called out or exposed.
- They know your friends will be honest with you and, they will therefore avoid any situation in which they cannot control.
- They want to control what others know about you, and will do it when you are not around. This will set you up to be undermined by your own network.
- They do not want you to continue to have friends, especially solid friends who will speak truth and love and care for you genuinely.
- They want to cause a segregation.
- They will put down your friends, so you see them less, call them less, choose to forego the relationship altogether, so they will have more control in your life. With less people that you look to for advice or assistance in time of need, it increases the likelihood that you will stay in the abusive situation.

The narcissist wants to keep you in the relationship, so they can continue the abuse cycle. They want your support network to dry up so you are reliant upon them and are unable to leave the relationship. They want to isolate you from your friends, companions, colleagues, anyone that has influence in your life, that could support you in a time of need during or after the relationship ends. Why? Because it's all about them. It is not about the relationship, and it has never been. This is a hard pill to swallow. The narcissist intentions with the relationship were not true, they didn't care for you like they said they would. It's all about them, and what they could receive from it.

Causes a Disturbance

Another tactic a narcissist uses to alienate you from your friends is to cause a disturbance before you are about to leave to meet up for a fun event with your friends.

They start an incredible argument.

Let's do another hypothetical situation, plans cancelled as a result:

1. Argument Started by the Narcissist
2. You try to keep the peace, defend the accusation, but the argument gets worse and escalates.
3. You agree to fix the issue, work on yourself (as the narcissist says you are to blame) so the situation de-escalates.
4. You cancel your event with your friends as you are emotionally disturbed by the argument.

Should you continue the fun event with your friends, this is the scenario:

1. Argument Started by the Narcissist
2. You try to keep the peace, defend the accusation, but the argument gets worse.
3. You continue to go to the event but your partner sends demanding texts all throughout the evening.
4. Partner asks for immediate responses.
5. Partner threatens in text.
6. Partner calls non-stop.
7. Partner falsely accuses your whereabouts.
8. Partner accuses you of lying (even if you have time-stamped pictures, etc.)
9. Claims you don't love them, and other false claims, and intensity increases.

10. Your story is never enough. No matter how much you relay the truth and have evidence to support, it will not suffice.
11. When you come home ready to discuss with your partner, after they have been calling and sending you messages all night, partner is sleeping and has nothing to say.
12. They claim the events of your fun night are in your head (gaslighting), the argument you had before you left the house was a simple question out of love and concern and, you blew it way out of proportion.

This calls for you to question your sanity, as you suffer through the gaslighting and cognitive dissonance, trying to make sense of it all. You evaluate all that has happened, over and over again, trying to understand. Your partner denies anything happened, has no remorse, laughs off your disgust with their behavior and lives another day. Sleeps soundly while you are emotionally wrecked.

The next time your friends ask to meet up, you decline without any further consideration as you cannot emotionally afford to go through this again. This fertilizes the soil with the seeds they have planted so emotional isolation can grow.

Monopolizing Conversations

The narcissist answers for you because they feel threatened at what you might share. They must be in control of what you say and even how you say it. The narcissist is afraid that you will share the truth in your relationship. They want to be the voice of the relationship to control the information others have.

The victim of abuse may be honest, which may not put them in the best light. When your partner responds, they control the dissemination of information. They will put their spin on it to bring the glory back to themselves.

- Do you find that your partner answers for you consistently?

- Are you unable to share your opinions to others while they are by your side?
- Do they interrupt and talk over you and share your side of the story?
- Do you feel like you can't get a word in on conversations? Are you cut off, or interrupted over and over again?

While they answer for you, many times they will also gaslight you at the same time.

Oh, "She loves it!" they will say. They silence you into submission.

If you choose to override them, and correct them in public and say, "No, I really feel this way…" after they have already told the audience how you feel, there will be revenge. Perhaps, they will now begin to mock you, all in jest of course, and play it off like it's no big deal.

The narcissist will be so angry that you have countered, that you shared your own opinion, or one that is contrary, or even to slightly correct and speak your mind, that they will train you so you do not speak, out of alignment again.

In a healthy relationship, there is mutual listening and sharing of feelings. When in a relationship with a narcissist, not only do they answer for you, they tell you what you should think and feel. The narcissist wants to control the conversation, and by control this means oftentimes not allowing you have the opportunity to speak and get a word in.

When they shut you down it's an attempt for them to re-gain control of the conversation, and, it may exacerbate your self-doubt. You may think that the narcissist knows best and therefore, it was a good catch that they interrupted or you may have made a fool out of yourself.

They want to brainwash you to not speak up, to lose your voice, lose your independent thought and to crush your spirit. They want you to feel less than, not worthy and just give up, and give in, to their control and allow them to handle things.

Again, people interrupt conversations, what we are looking for in this instance is the repeated monopolizing of conversation and interruption, repeatedly cutting you off so you are unable to share. The keyword here is repeated, ongoing, often, over and over again, obtuse behavior.

Listening to Find Weak Spots

When in a relationship with a narcissist, and when we share our heart, are open and vulnerable to share our deep secrets, beware! The narcissist saves these conversations and puts them in their mind for later use. They will bring up these very personal events, thoughts, opinions all to use against us a later time. The narcissist will twist them around in some defaming angle to cause humiliation.

Mind Games

A narcissist's favorite games are the ones they can play with you, especially mind games. They are deliberate and very controlled. The narcissist will orchestrate conversations, to drive you crazy. They are to wear down your self-esteem, your abilities, your thoughts, everything. They are meant to confuse and to obliterate your peace.

They play these mind games so you will question who you are, and take your eyes off them. They want to be viewed as the super-hero, who knows what is best for you at all times.

Circular Conversations

The narcissists favorite hobby is to cause a distraction to coincide with their avoidance of responsibility. A narcissist instigates conversations where not only the subject changes frequently, by their doing, but they insert false accusations, to get your attention so you try to clear up the scenario. They do not intend to actually engage in a form of communication that resolves issues.

Their intent is to confuse, and dismantle effective communication. They don't want to resolve, and be held accountable. They will not answer direct questions. They can be fast talkers and have become masters at verbal manipulation with charisma. They bounce from topic to topic with ease including accusatory language, while we are left with a horrible pit in our stomach. We have the notion, that things are so off base, but can't get a word into the conversation and the subject keeps changing. Unresolved conversations from months ago are thrown in to add layers to the pile. Nothing is resolved and this is deliberate.

Have you had 6 conversations going at the same time in 5 minutes? If so, you probably have had a conversation with a narcissist.

The narcissist will orchestrate circular conversations to cause confusion. These conversations try to get us to play first, second and third base, plus be the outfielder all in a short time span. They have you running all over the place and designed so you can't get a word in and are constantly running trying to play damage control. They are hitting the ball and blaming you that you cannot carry on a conversation like a decent human being!

Of course, if you decide to have a conversation and discuss many subjects, which do connect, and are relevant in the normal chain of a conversation, they will say that you are all over the place. My point is they will accuse of the very thing they do and then will deny it!

Minimize

Minimizing is the art of coercion to lower someone else's reality. It's a manipulation tactic that tries to reduce the full implicated value of a concern. Have you presented a need in your relationship and then your partner dismissed it then placated you? This a form of minimizing you and your thoughts. Here's a hypothetical example:

You say: "We should hug more!"

Partner Response: "Hugs are overrated!"

They minimize, belittle and devalue you all with a few words.

- Does the narcissist say things like you are overacting?
- Are you accused of making a mountain out of molehill?
- Do they say you always blow everything out of proportion?

The narcissist is minimizing your concern and is trying to control you and what you should think! They also want to silence you and make you feel ashamed for raising your concern, while raising their feeling of superiority (Minimizing: A Form of Control 2017). They are being dismissive and purposefully not giving the concern the weight and attention, it deserves.

If you have an argument and are deeply hurt and discuss it with the narcissist, they will justify and excuse their behavior. They will even say, "Was it really that bad?"

The constant minimizing, has the victim questioning themselves. They say, "Was it really that bad, am I overacting? Maybe I shouldn't have said anything...."

The narcissist is training the victim to lose their footing and to question their own reality. The victim is getting brainwashed by the narcissist, and their reality is continually being modified based on the emotional abuse.

When these manipulative tactics are used on the victim, many times the victim does not see or even believe they are being manipulated. They victim of abuse goes along with what the narcissist says. They turn on themselves. They work harder in trying to improve the relationship. They step it up. The bear the responsibility of the relationship and believe what the narcissist says.

The narcissist loves this willingness of their partner to work things out and this ideology is the very skillset they are attacking.

3rd Parties Added for Jealousy /Triangulation

The narcissist can and will use any other party in a triangulation against you, the mailman, the dentist, the office receptionist, best friend, neighbor, there is end to the web that they will build.

In romantic relationships a similar dynamic occurs when an individual brings in another party to create jealousy and discord. They will love-bomb the new individual while the current individual in the relationship is devalued. The narcissist may allow each party to know the other exists so they vie for the attention and affection of the narcissist. The narcissist enjoys the attention from both parties fighting over them.

Triangulation occurs when the narcissist pits people against each other. The stage is set when the narcissist introduces a third party with the deliberate intention to orchestrate drama and create jealousy between the parties. It breeds confusion and relational drama whilst the narcissist controls the information disseminated to the parties.

Sometimes the narcissist will make comments to stir things up and say things like, you don't do your hair like (the other party). The narcissist wants you to feel jealous, even insulted and focus on yourself instead of them.

Stonewalling

While engaging with a narcissist, you will find they will try to abruptly shut down conversations when they are not comfortable. They refuse to talk about whatever it is and they need to end the conversation right then in there. The following examples are when in an established relationship, general questions are asked, and the topics could be very simple questions, but the response is the same.

Have you heard the following?

- "This conversation is pointless!", and they walk away.
- "You are overreacting!"
- "You don't need to know that information."
- "I have no time for this."
- Or they just flat out say "No."

They do this to shut down the conversation. They don't and won't answer even basic questions.

What we are looking for is repeated patterns. One off's in a proper healthy environment are okay. We are seeking to identify tactics inside of a covert, manipulative emotionally abusive relationship.

Withholding Information/Generalized Statements

Many times, they not only avoid the direct questions, they refuse to answer, or will only partially answer, generating more questions. When asked, they will also leave out information so as you are not hearing the full story, which is withholding information.

A narcissist will lie, and try to cover up deceit. They won't be held to any questions for information. They refuse accountability. They will continue to deflect and refuse responsibility.

The tactics a narcissistic abuser uses are not one offs. They are repeated events that occur over and over again. Everyone can have a bad day and not perform at their best. That is not what we are talking about here. We are discussing the repeated obtuse deceitful behaviors.

Since a narcissist doesn't like to be held accountable, even for small "insignificant" things, when asked, they will have a whole host of defense mechanisms to distract, undermine and control you and your response to them.

They will withhold information. If you ask a question, they refuse to answer, or they even won't tell the full story. They are not forthright. If you ask your question a different way, you are likely to be faced with stonewalling. If they don't want to answer, they are not going to, and will shift into other tactics to avoid.

Violence

An emotional abuser's only tactics to manipulate you is not only through the mind. When tensions are high violent abuse often occurs.

- Each year, more than 3 million women in the U.S. are abused in a domestic violence partnership and 1,600 are killed by their abusers.
- Women are 70 times more likely to be killed in the two weeks after leaving a relationship than at any other time during the relationship (Mitchell, 2017).

When women leave a relationship, this is the time when tensions between parties have the highest chance of a violent encounter.

Please reach out the National Domestic Violence Hotline 1-800-799-7233 (English)/1-800-797-3224 (En Español) for assistance and/or contact local authorities if you are in immediate danger.

Intimidation

A narcissistic emotional abuser will intimidate you to get you to operate under their control. They will intimidate through fear. Some examples they will use is body stance, facial expressions that show their disapproval. They will raise their voice, scream and yell. They bully and threaten. These are all methods to get you to back down from them and change your behavior to get back in alignment.

Playing Victim

In a conversation with a narcissist, if you try to explain how you feel about a subject, they will switch gears into being the victim.

They have the poor-me mentality. After a breakup or divorce, they perpetuate themselves as the one with devasting loss. "She left me." They see themselves as a victim to garner support; however, they are the ones inflicting the pain.

Blaming you

One of the key features of a narcissist, is their inability to take responsibility. They are masters of blame-shifting in conversations.

- I did this because you…
- If only you were (a better cook), I wouldn't be forced to do (fill in the blank) …
- I have to (fill in the blank) because you …
- I can't work because you don't….

False Accusations/Projections

An emotional abuser will accuse others often of the very things they are doing. This is called projections. They project onto their target what they are doing.

- Does your partner accuse you or having an extramarital affair?
- Does your partner accuse you of being secretive?
- Does your partner accuse you of lying and not telling the full story?
- Does your partner accuse you of small insignificant things over and over again?

They want you to take the bait and become defensive.

Brainwashing

The narcissist wants to get into your head. They will train you to behave how they need you to respond. This starts from the onset of the relationship. They are reviewing your skills, and ability to think for yourself, be independent, be successful, empathy and the like. It's a game for the narcissist to find someone successful and on top of their game.

The narcissist will brainwash their victims so they obey, and lose sight of their goals and objectives, dreams and visions. They do this slowly and one bite at a time, and when you are dependent upon them, they discard. The lower the narcissist can bring you, the more elevated and powerful they feel.

Starting an Argument but at First, Just a Conversation

Many times, a narcissist will start a conversation out of manufactured concern. They *appear* they want to work on the relationship, and *appear* to be genuine so you take the bait. Then, once you take the relationship drama bait, the conversation escalates and they throw out accusatory language, and you defend. They make statements on how defensive you are and that you are the reason why the relationship is messed up. They claim they cannot talk to you since you are so defensive and they can't get a word in edgewise. This conversation just circles around.

Constant High Criticism

The criticism can start out slow and it may appear to be simple feedback. What makes the criticism stand out from ordinary criticism, is that it's highly critical and often. It's on another level and many times it's about little mundane things. The criticisms can be from anything, small big, trivial or not. The narcissist looks for things to criticize about.

You have a kind heart to work on things to reinstate peace. You work on the issues they complain about. The thing is once you have corrected the issue and aim to please, it is never enough, and the carrot moves and the constant criticism continues.

What is uncanny is that if there is perceived criticism toward something they did or did not do, they cannot handle it and will lash back.

Appearance of No Knowledge of Common Social Skills

Do you feel like you need to train someone in your life how to act with regard to common social skills? These can be simple tasks and traits and relationship standards.

"Oh, I didn't know that you would be offended if I had lunch with Mary, you never told me. I thought you liked Mary!"

The narcissist will "pretend" they were not aware of certain things and is infamous for flipping the script. They will blame you for their infraction.

Forgetful of Birthdays/Special Occasions

Dare you speak up that you should have a card or a gift or treated special for your birthday or special occasion and you wish you never said anything. According to the narcissist, you don't deserve to be treated special. It's not about you, it's about them.

At the same time, when you take your partner out for a special occasion to celebrate, they will put it down and say we are going here? Why would you think this would be something I wanted to do? It will never be enough.

The Narcissistic Rage

The narcissistic rage is fierce rage that can come out of nowhere. It's something that after experiencing one time, you don't want to experience it ever again.

The onset is unpredictable. Anything can set the narcissist off, a look, a comment, your reaction. It is as if all of the hate, anguish, fury that is inside comes to a boiling point and lets loose. The rage takes over and it is over-the-top frightening.

The rage is meant to intimidate and to get you to walk on egg-shells all while second guessing your every move.

False Apologies

The narcissist as we have stated earlier does not oblige with being responsible for his own actions. They dismiss them as no big deal due to their lack of empathy. Therefore, when you seek their reckoning with truth and to be held accountable for what offense they have caused, they will send a false apology.

Have you heard the following?

- "I am so sorry you feel that way."
- "I am sorry you think I did that."

It may sound like an apology. They are hoping you will buy it. They are hoping since the word, sorry, is in the sentence that it placates you. They are hoping it satisfies you and therefore will stop pestering them for a true heartfelt apology with changed behavior.

It's not a true apology. They simply mouthed the words. They have no intention to change anything and has deflected from taking responsibility for the infraction.

They have in the very same sentence, put the responsibility on you. They are saying *what you feel* is wrong (whatever the issue is). They are not saying I am sorry for what I have done. They deflect.

Lack of Validation

In a healthy conversation, there is both the listening and speaking elements of a conversation. When the conversation changes as both parties interact, commonly there is validation, which is letting the other party know they have been heard. Its respectful and it generates an atmosphere in which conversation can flow freely since both parties feel like they have been heard, and the exchange can form a healthy bond, even if parties do not agree on a topic. When in relationship with a narcissist, the element of validation is missing.

When seeking validation on a topic, the narcissist will not provide. They will pretend they did not hear you. They may ignore your request altogether. They will override your question or statement which calls for their input and put the focus back on themselves. So, you ask again, perhaps you ask in a different way, clearer to obtain a response, maybe they didn't hear you? At second pass, still no validation. The subject has now been deliberately changed, a diversion tactic.

So, now you have to think if you have to try to re-phrase a third time or just give up and let it go. That is exactly what the narcissist wants you to do. They don't want you pestering them (that is how they view it) with questions they may be held accountable for answering, no matter how big or small. They will be dismissive of your request and will ignore you. Later on, they will even claim you never said anything and that you should have brought up the subject. They are gaslighting and manipulating you.

The relationship quickly breaks down due to lack of validation. The victim feels like they have not been heard, which increases feelings of unworthiness, and creates lack of self-confidence. The lack of validation in communication, further silences the victim. They don't wish to speak up anymore. Silence then becomes preferred and the narcissist has trained their victim to keep quiet. The abuser can continue to abuse. It's a win for the narcissist, but devastating to the victim.

The narcissist is unable to form a bond, a solid connection with you that is imperative in intimate relationships. They cannot and will not validate your concerns, which isolates and alienates you in the relationship. Your thoughts and desire to connect, is of no concern to the narcissist. They are not there for your needs. They are not looking to build a solid relationship built on trust and mutual responsibility, respect and sharing.

Narcissists are master manipulators. They have mastered their trade through the years to perfect it.

No Empathy

One of the main characteristics of the narcissist, is the inability to empathize. They may fake empathy with words they have been taught, but it's not genuine. Their lack of empathy is evident when they are unable to see things from another's perspective continually. They only from see from their vantage point. The narcissist lacks compassion, true care and concern, and connecting from the heart is completely absent (remember the MRI Brain Scans from Chapter 1).

Lies

The narcissist lies to you to control the knowledge you have; this is a form of gaslighting. They are habitual and chronic liars from the moment they wake up to the moment they fall asleep. They are untrustworthy, and do not want to get caught in their own lies. If they are asked questions, they will use other tactics to avoid a response, lie, or cause a distraction. They have mastered the art of bullying to perpetuate their deceit. They lie cleverly to avoid getting caught, and if found out will deny the action. They will claim not to remember previous conversations, then, they will blame you for it.

A narcissist has a whole repertoire of tactics at their disposal and they use them continually on their targets. There is no way to win by overpowering their game. One only way to win, is to remove yourself from their harm. We will discuss this more in upcoming chapters.

Controlling the Finances

Narcissists have several ways in which they can control you through finances in a partner/marriage relationship. There is more to be said on the topic, but a brief overlay includes:

- They won't talk about money.
- They shut down the conversation when money is discussed.
- They will not contribute to household expenses.
- They will not let you know how much they make or
- They make 100% of the money and only give you a small portion to live on.
- If you are the breadwinner, they may not work even though they should, which causes undue financial stress and pressure on the relationship.
- They may not allow you to have access to retirement accounts, or checking accounts.
- They pay all the bills and don't treat you as an equal partner and decision-maker in the budget.
- They may not add you to the title/deed/mortgage.
- They buy large purchases without checking with you.
- They have other financial accounts that they deny having.
- If one partner is the primary bread winner, and the spouse has less income, they still require 50/50 split on bills. They are not open to even discussing the idea of restructuring the percentages for proper contributions (Hammond, 2015).

The narcissist wants to destroy your credit, not give you access to money, even in its rightfully yours so that you will not have the means to get out the relationship. It's a way that he tries to trap you, preventing you being able to escape, by controlling the finances.

Takers in a Relationship

A healthy relationship has a steady balance between give and take. In relationship with a narcissist, they are the takers. They keep on taking without replenishing. The narcissist will withdraw funds from your emotional bank account without depositing funds to keep it afloat.

Everything is a withdrawal, until the relationship goes back to the love-bombing stage. Many victims of narcissistic abuse, wait for the love-bombing stage to recirculate. They try harder, aim to please, and try to fix issues in the relationship, but nothing works. The narcissist, will require more and more supply. The love-bomb stage is just a false front, to re-hook their target and to reel them back in.

- Are you seeing these tactics in your relationship?
- Are you seeing these patterns over and over?

Thus far, we have discussed 33 tactics narcissists use on their targets to manipulate, deceive and control. While this list is not exhaustive, it establishes the groundwork to which we can use as a guidebook to discern if we are in an emotionally abusive relationship. Hopefully these tactics will shed light and provide insight.

One of the tools often discussed to begin the healing journey after narcissistic abuse, is to draw the line. This line, is the No Contact Line. This is literally to have no further contact with the abuser, some even refer to it as grey rock, which is similar. No contact is no contact, no text, no phone calls, no holiday visits, while grey rock is to low contact, without emotional involvement and is typically in place if there is a reason for communication to remain in short stints.

No contact, is a big decision and is to be carefully thought about, especially if this is the first time hearing of this method to start the healing journey.

By going no contact with an abuser, there is no need to make an announcement, it an action, by our choosing, that helps to put an end to the emotional abuse, and to begin to rebuild. No contact is the beginning....

NO CONTACT IS THE BEGINNING

After learning the traits, mindset and mental disposition of the narcissistic emotional abuser, and deciding to go no contact, or grey rock, this step is the beginning of the process into healing and recovery, and is a carefully thought-out decision.

There is not one strategy to overcome narcissistic abuse from emotional manipulators as the journey can look different for everyone; however, what occurs after no contact, or grey rock, is the biggest rebuilding effort of your life. It's the journey to self-discovery, introspection and the time to rise. It's the journey to stake your ground, to take inventory of your life, friends, acquaintances, family relationships, all of it, and be willing to make changes.

This means, we may need to re-evaluate where we live, even our job situation, to whether or not we choose to engage with certain family members or friends, our marriage. We do not have to take the abuse. We were not meant to endure abuse of any kind.

We may have grown accustomed to the abuse, not only that, but for some, it may be all we have known. Taking steps to make a change, can absolutely be frightening and there is a world of unknowns for the future. This is where is can become an all-out war for our survival. We may have been in a relationship with this person for years, decades, or grown up in a situation. By going no contact, we are in essence, shutting the door to the abuse from happening, but again, but it's the beginning. No contact may mean moving to another location, moving out, quitting a job and finding a new one, and/or leaving a marriage.

As you think about your situation, and evaluate relationships, the steps that follow, will be gradual. You may have a notion of what your next step is, and again, it's the beginning. Continue to plan, and think things through. Enlist a support network with individuals you can trust with your life, and engage with appropriate counselors who specialize in narcissistic abuse, and learn all you can in the meantime.

We cannot control another person, what we are responsible for is our reaction and the choices we make from that point forward. Narcissistic abusers will not change. They just modify their tactics of manipulation to keep it in tact.

It's important to learn not only about the process of establishing no contact, but to learn about the grieving and loss that occurs afterward. It's like grieving the death of a spouse or loved one, yet they are alive and can still cause harm, and many do, even after no contact. They will infiltrate a smear campaign to cause your reputation to be harmed; as their abuse tries to continue behind the scenes. By establishing a "no contact" boundary it draws a line in the sand, so you can grieve the loss and begin to move forward.

Grief and Loss After No Contact

Few understand the deep grief and loss that occurs after choosing to implement a "no contact" resolution following narcissistic abuse. Some may think, why would you have anything to grieve about? They were abusive. You are free. Now what?

It is so much more than that.

There are layers of grief and deep processing of events, thoughts, mindsets, unpacking and sorting through the stories and events that were told, that were once believed.

Sifting through the past can bring freedom and release as the truth clearly unfolds; however, at the same time, going through the loss can surface pain and a feeling of wasted time and years believing in what was false. For this, there is grieving the loss of everything that was and is, and was meant to be, or that never was, or should have never been.

It takes time, even years, to digest the loss from a relationship. Loss occurs in stages with variance in between the stages, it's not a linear path. There may be mixed emotions, anger, hurt, devastation to sort through. There is no rush in healing. The journey can take a while, but it's important to be an active participant in the recovery process.

A flower blooms in the field – even if no one is there to see it.

The process of loss, can be slow, but it's the choice to be free and to no longer be subjected to the abuse, and from there it starts the rebuilding efforts. The process consists of deeply grieving the loss down to the root in various stages. The grieving process takes time as there are years to unpack and sort through. It may mean grieving 20-year relationships or more, reminiscing prior conversations, prior motives as the truth continues to unfold.

Moreover, the vast rebuilding effort is wide in that it impacts, in essence, all relationships, from family to friendships, even colleagues, to partner/spouse relationships. It leaves no stone unturned. This is where few understand the gravity of the loss involved. You may end up grieving the loss of an abusive relationship, plus friendships and family members, not to mention moving, changing jobs, and the like. It's a massive rebuilding effort to remove the toxicity that was unknown, which is now realized.

The escape from narcissistic, emotional, physical, spiritual abuse is difficult for many victims. The abused definitely goes into a survival mentality, goes into flight-or-fight mode, while juggling and overcoming the hurdles along the way.

When we remove manipulators, it opens the door for new relationships to form, and new pathways to be formed. It's like a new highway is being built, as there is the process of clearing away of the old road debris. The rebuilding efforts take time, but it may just be what the doctor ordered.

Does narcissistic abuse outside of relationships? Does it occur within corporations, associations or even within governments? What about social media? Does Hollywood favor narcissistic character types in popular movies? Let's explore narcissism on a broader scale.

GLOBAL NARCISSISM

If you repeat a lie often enough, people will believe it, and you will even come to believe it yourself. (Joseph Goebbels)

Thus far, we have discussed the methods narcissistic abusers use to control their victims in search for their own narcissistic supply. Narcissists portray a false image that they are caring, empathetic, and are typically well-liked by the general population; however, underneath this false image lies a devious, corrupted individual and are only after their own objectives at any cost. The bounds of narcissism absolutely exist within interpersonal relationships as we have laid out, now let's take a moment to view narcissism on a broader, even global scale beginning with current trends in social media.

Social Media and Narcissism

Many people state there is a rise of narcissism due to social media. While this may the recent trend, there is more to the story. The spirit of narcissism, is not new, it's been around for a long time and even stories of it back in the Bible. Today, we are seeing the fruit of this devastating disorder now more than ever before. Narcissists love to use social media platforms to exploit others for their personal gain. It's another avenue. It's a resource and a source of supply for them.

With the prevalence of social media; we are seeing the increase of this disorder more than ever before, but can it occur on a more global scale? Can it occur within governments and corporate institutions? Let's switch gears a bit and dive in briefly.

Corporate Level Control

David Cain in his article, <u>Your Lifestyle Has Already been Designed"</u> writes on the 8-hour workday which many corporations support and adhere. Cain provides a perspective after he completed an extended trip and is refreshingly quoted saying the following; my additions are in brackets:

> But the 8-hour workday is too profitable for big business, not because of the amount of work people get done in eight hours (the average office worker gets less than three hours of actual work done is 8 hours) but because it makes for such a purchase-happy public. Keeping free time scarce means people pay a lot more for convenience, gratification, and any other relief they can buy. It keeps them watching television [propaganda], and its commercials. It keeps them unambitious [lack of goals, dreams, visions, living our true purpose] outside of work. We've been led into a culture that has been engineered to leave us tired, hungry for indulgence, willing to pay a lot for convenience and entertainment, and most importantly, vaguely dissatisfied with our lives so that we continue wanting things we don't have. We buy so much because it always seems like something is still missing (Cain, 2014).

Have we been led to believe that we must live a certain life? Have we been trained to think about how we should live our life, spend our time and money?

Has there been a plan for our life, *designed by others*, before we were born?

Are we taught the following as an acceptable pattern for life?

1. Go to college.
2. Get into vast amounts of student loan debt.
3. Get a corporate job, work 8 hours, get promoted so you can work more and have more responsibility, so you can get paid more so you can get out of debt.
4. Get married.
5. Have 2.2 kids.
6. Make a lot of money.

7. Buy a house, a large one.
8. Spend your free time fixing up the home and making it look wonderful to impress your friends to show you have made it.
9. Collect as many toys as you can possibly fit into your house to convince yourself and, of course others, that you have finally made it.
10. Have an amazing lawn with no weeds.
11. Work until you are 65 or later.

If there is any deviation and independent thought apart from the concept and "plan for your life", many will try to get you back in alignment with the beliefs that we should have.

Dare to think for yourself, and choose a different path and not only will many of your friends and acquaintances think you have gone mad, but society will not paint you in a positive light.

Dare to engage in your own agenda, and plan your own life adventure outside of the system and create your own personal belief system and try to carry it to fruition and you will be met with strong opposing counterparts. Why is this so? Think about the influence media and corporate culture has on us. Is there a certain level of control within these institutions, and if you believe the answer is yes, why do you think this is so? What do corporations have to gain by controlling us? What about governments; do they use the power of control and manipulation?

Nazi Germany and the Propaganda Machine

Joseph Goebbels was a German politician and Reich Minister of Propaganda of Nazi Germany from 1933 to 1945. He was one of Adolf Hitler's closest and devoted associates. He was *master orator* and he was the orchestrator of the Nazi propaganda machine and brought to fruition its devious master agenda.

According to Britannica, the definition of propaganda is "dissemination of information – facts, arguments, rumors, half-truths, or lies – to influence public opinion." (Smith, 2020)

Do you believe there is still propaganda today? If so, how do you see this play out in society today?

As we see manipulation occurring within relationships, sometimes we have to take a step back and see the same tactics are occurring elsewhere. Again, the tactics are not new, time has just allowed tactics to become perfected – and even more devious.

Do you see manipulation and deception occurring from a broader even global scale? What about Hollywood movies? Does Hollywood play a role with the spirit of narcissism indirectly?

Movies with Narcissistic Roles Glorified

Hollywood is at the center of the innocuous attempt to create generalized acceptance of narcissistic characters in movies, and sitcoms. Let's take a look at some examples, there are many more, but here are a few:

The Devil Wears Prada (2006): A writer (played by Anne Hathaway) who acquires a position as Editor-in-Chief to a fashion magazine, working for a tyrannical boss (played by Meryl Streep).

Anchorman: The Legend of Ron Burgundy (2004): Comedy starring Will Ferrell who feels threatened by a new ambitious anchorwoman joining the set.

Mommie Dearest (1981): Infamous real-life story of narcissist Joan Crawford (played by Faye Dunaway) and the horror she created for her daughter Christina.

You (2019): Series Description: "A dangerously charming, intensely obsessive young man (Joe Golberg) goes to extreme measures to insert himself into the lives of those he is transfixed by."

Everybody Loves Raymond (1996-2005): The character, Marie (Doris Roberts), plays the mother-in-law bully. She guilt-trips, criticizes, minimizes and accuses others of being too-sensitive; characteristic traits of emotional abuse and narcissism (Top 10 Favorite Narcissistic Characters. 2010).

While there are more movies that we could list as examples, what is noteworthy is narcissism may not just occur within interpersonal relationships. It's important to see narcissism can also occur on a global scale. Once the onion starts to peel and we can see the layers unfold within relationships, sometimes we can see the same exact patterns and tactics used broadly. Sometimes the tactics are deeply embedded within the culture, it's hard to see. It's necessary to widen our lens to see the traits discussed in the book in other relational aspects.

Next, I'm going to share a little bit about my background and personal story.

An Interesting Perspective

My Background

Over 20 years ago, I graduated from a Christian University with a 4-year degree to pursue missions. Then, I felt a desire to be a missionary and share God's word to the nations. After graduating, I never entered the mission field directly, even though I completed a summer internship in South Africa after my junior year. I always felt like I missed the boat, in that 20 years has gone by from the days of hermeneutics and eschatology. The thought and the stirring of it has been present with me since this time. I remember the days fondly, the friendships that were born, and the many memories that were created.

Though I was prepared to embark on the mission solo, it never occurred, and I entered the corporate world and got married at age 40 for the first time.

3 Month Honeymoon

My husband and I had what I will call, the three-month honeymoon. Things were wonderful, well sort of, but then my husband picked a fight about something minor, and carried the same argument for the next 6 months or so.

Then he became increasingly angry at simple things out of nowhere. We had circular conversations that would not get resolved, though I tried desperately to settle, so we could come to an agreement and move on. There was blame-shifting and a high-level of constant criticism. His moods would change in an instant, and I began to walk on eggshells, not knowing what the heck happened. The relationship was taking a rapid turn, but I still had hope.

Now, of course, the relationship did not start out like this. When we were dating, I believed I saw the fruits of his hand, as he was involved in many ministries in the church and appeared to live the Christian lifestyle. He was outspoken with his extended family with causes for the Lord, and spoke about how heart-broken he was for some members of his family.

He laid the land that he wanted his close friends and family all to come to a full knowledge and heartfelt relationship with God. He quoted Scripture like I have never seen anyone do before, even in my years at college. Many of his friends told him he should be a pastor. His response was that he had been a Christian for 30 years, and he believed that's what a Christian should do.

Divorce was not an option; we were going to make it, so I thought. I believed it with my whole heart. I felt that there is nothing God cannot do. I knew many couples and especially newlyweds go through a period of acclimation in the first few years of marriage and I was prepared for this time of adaptation, even though we had known each other for over 8 years.

I had the mindset to work through things with diligence, patience, and with an expectant heart of a positive outcome; however, stress and anxiety were building in the relationship. I tried to fix things, work harder, be sweeter, and I took on more responsibility in the marriage with the hope to try to work things out. I loved him and wanted us to succeed.

Too, I was rapidly changing in the relationship. I was taking on more and more responsibility and the more I took on, the more imbalance it created.

At the time, I thought that if I took on more, it would balance things out. I was wrong, so wrong. My naivety was staring me in the face.

Departure

When I started to see patterns unfold on a repeated basis in my marriage, I began to make changes. I didn't announce my changes, but I gradually changed my behavior to suit and further test out my situation. As I began to make slight changes, this is when the relationship escalated.

What ensued was a domestic disturbance. The abuse went from emotional to physical. I had to leave. I left at 11:30 PM after a disturbance. The cops were called. The line was crossed for the last time. I took my dignity and drove off to stay at a friend's house. I took with me a few items as I departed, along with my dog.

I knew I was going to be okay. I knew I was going to make it.

I felt in a weird way that the Lord was telling me to go. I took a leap of faith and knew it was time to leave. When I left my home for the last time, I knew I was doing the right thing, even though many in the "Christian" circles, would have told me not to do so, as some even did.

The message taught in the Christian circles, is to try harder, pray more, be sweeter, amongst other things. And, because this message is taught in the church behind closed doors in counseling, and even indirectly from the pulpit, this is when I began to question further this aspect of my denomination.

If my denomination taught that it's okay for one partner to abuse the other and for it to be acceptable, I had to make some changes. This is absolutely unacceptable. This is the whistleblower message, that they do not want spoken about. This book will probably not make it to the top 10 books recommended by pastors or churches, but it's a message that needs to heard. There are victims suffering in silence, many confused, many in fear, and many needing hope and encouragement with their situation.

In an emotionally abusive relationship, trying harder, being sweeter, only creates an atmosphere for additional abuse to be imparted.

When I left, I was saying goodbye to my marriage. Even though I wanted it to work, I had to make a decision, if I was going to remain in an unhealthy marriage for the sake of appearances and from what my denomination taught, or if I was going to put myself in a healthy environment.

In an escalated situation as such, there will be no shortage of people encouraging you to stay – even in the interim. It's completely backwards. I remember one pastor, who we sought counseling from, claimed that I was upset with beard trimmings in the sink, without asking questions to truly ascertain the situation. This was by no means the issue, and it was a way to not only minimize the situation, but for me to stay.

I left it all behind. I had clothes for about a week, and few other items.

I had no idea this move was the catapult to going into low lows and hitting my future rock bottom, only to survive and go through some rough hurdles to make it over the mountain. Sometimes I am not sure If I have made it over the mountain, or if I am still climbing, but I am moving forward and ahead, learning every day.

There is more to my story. I have been there.

The relationship I had with my ex-husband, was the caveat for me to make changes, and massive changes. I have gone no contact with some members of my family to include extended family and friends. I had to make radical, personal changes.

As stated earlier, when women leave a relationship, this is the time when tensions between parties have the highest chance of a violent encounter.

- Each year, more than 3 million women in the U.S. are abused in a domestic violence partnership and 1,600 are killed by their abusers.

- Women are 70 times more likely to be killed in the two weeks after leaving a relationship than at any other time during the relationship (Mitchell, 2017).

If leaving your relationship is the best course of action, please have a plan in place to work through the risk levels, so you can land on your feet the best way possible. Get a supportive network together so you will have access to a team of people who can assist. I plan to continue to provide resources on our website, Moving Forward with Hope

(https://www.movingforwardafterabuse.com/), to include: a corresponding workbook, to work through narcissistic abuse with a guidebook and an action plan with steps to gather resources from all angles to be best prepared to make a move, should you decide that the course for you.

Emotional abuse absolutely occurs within Christian homes. It occurs in husband-wife/romantic partnerships, as well as within Parent/Child families. I make the distinction, since within the Christian sector, is where the silence behind it is so strong. In addition, there are tactics the church has set in place to keep many women in emotionally abusive marriages, which I may delve into at a later time. More and more people are speaking up, and in that, many churches, and pastors want this message to remain behind closed doors, so they can control the opinions of others, and to reframe it as what is best for the church, within the delicate framework of evangelical ministry.

There's More and This is Going to Get Real

As I was learning about narcissistic abuse while married, one thought would surface from time to time. It had to do with my now ex-husband's mother. She was my mother-in-law, but we never met, you see, she was in an emotionally devastating marriage for decades and she died by suicide a very long time ago, over 30 years ago.

I mention this as I believe if I didn't leave the relationship I was in, I was headed in the same direction. Now, let me provide some additional clarification. In my life, I never thought about suicide. It never came to my mind. My point is this, being exposed to narcissistic abuse for years, decades, many view suicide as the only way out of the constant pain (Jack, 2020).

Being exposed to narcissistic abuse, is emotionally damaging, so if this is you, let me encourage you to talk to a professional today who can assist with your situation.

There is absolutely hope, and once out of an abusive relationship, the mind can clear and the situation gets better, absolutely better.

National Suicide Prevention Lifeline 1-800-273-8255, available 24/7.

New Perspective

I went to Bible college, graduated, was going to pursue giving years of my life to live overseas sharing the message of the Bible to complete strangers. Even though I have worked in corporate America for the past 20 years and had a mission in my heart, it has changed. The mission has morphed into this mission, to be a resource of hope, restoration, and validation for those who are in, or who were in, emotionally abusive situations, whether it be family or marriage, or friends.

There are many who are faced with decisions to make. Perhaps you are in an abusive relationship, but have nowhere to turn. You see yourself in the tactics we have reviewed. You have been silenced for decades for fear in facing the deep roots that have grown in your life, that may need to be ripped out.

I am in my mid 40's. I divorced my husband and birth family, and legally changed my first and last name, after I saw the layers of the onion fall off. I lost friends, but what I gained was the truth, and it changed my world.

You know your story. It's unique to your situation. I am here to support and encourage you on your journey. Please see our website for additional resources to assist in recovering from narcissistic abuse, Moving Forward with Hope. The site is to serve as a resource of hope, encouragement and validation to victims of narcissistic abuse, so lives can be rebuilt by facilitating a revolutionary change to pursue dreams, visions and living intentionally. Validation. Rebuild. Revolutionize.

https://www.movingforwardafterabuse.com/

CONCLUSION

Narcissism, is not new, has been around for quite some time. It is estimated that approximately 6% or over 19 million people living in the U.S. have Narcissistic Personality Disorder, and globally over 468 million people. The impact of this disorder is wide and many have been impacted.

The tactics are devious, underhanded, often discreet to not be detected. Narcissists love to fly under the radar so they can continue to extract supply from their victims continually. While serving as master manipulators, narcissists engage in obtuse behavior to fill their need or narcissistic supply until their next target provides. These emotional abusers have become masters of their trade and leave a devastating path behind them.

By becoming keen to the abuse cycle, and learning their behaviors, we can detect, discover and choose our response so to not be controlled, manipulated or deceived.

No Contact is just the beginning of choosing to draw a line and put a stop to the abuse. It's a decision to be carefully evaluated to discern the right move, backed with a support network to assist on the journey.

When we witness manipulation occurring within interpersonal relationships, we can also widen our perspective to see similar traits of narcissism globally and within some organizations.

I want to thank you for downloading this book. If you have received value and have benefited from the information contained, I would appreciate if you could leave a positive review so others can benefit from the information as well. Thank you.

Click here to leave your review.

ABOUT THE AUTHOR

Lynn Nichols, narcissistic abuse recovery coach, survivor and author of: *Overcoming the Devastation of Narcissistic Abuse: How to Heal, Recover and Take Your Life Back, and 49 Powerhouse Affirmations: Rejuvenate your Soul and Mind after a Destructive Relationship.* Lynn is passionate to be a resource of hope, encouragement and validation to victims of narcissistic abuse, especially women, so lives can be rebuilt by facilitating a revolutionary change to pursue dreams, visions, and living intentionally.

Moving Forward with Hope. Validate. Rebuild. Revolutionize.

Please also check out our website: https://movingforwardafterabuse.com/

Send us an email: info@movingforwardafterabuse.com

Sign up and subscribe to my mailing list, which is found on our website. Let's stay in contact.

Speaking Engagements:

If you wish to connect with me to speak, or share my story, or appear on a podcast, or want to send me a personal email, send me an email at Lynn@movingforwardafterabuse.com. Please give us 24-48 hours to respond.

Follow us on Social Media:

We choose the name Wake the Elephant, since for many, the elephant has been in the room so long, it fell asleep. Today is the day to Wake the Elephant.

YouTube: https://www.youtube.com/channel/UCj_u7tlSj2GKX-RxOuipB6g

Facebook: https://www.facebook.com/waketheelephant

Instagram: https://www.instagram.com/waketheelephant/

Pinterest: https://www.pinterest.com/waketheelephant/

Twitter: https://twitter.com/waketheelephant

49 POWERHOUSE AFFIRMATIONS: Rejuvenate your Soul and Mind after a Destructive Relationship

Click Here to Claim Your Free Copy

Other Books by Author

Overcoming the Devastation of Narcissistic Abuse: How to Heal, Recover and Take Your Life Back

49 POWERHOUSE Affirmations: Rejuvenate your Soul and Mind after a Destructive Relationship

Additional Resources

<u>Is it Me? Making Sense of Your Confusing Marriage? A Christian Woman's Guide to Hidden Emotional and Spiritual Abuse</u>

<u>Life Saving Divorce: Hope for People Leaving Destructive Relationships</u>

<u>Divorce: The Real Truth Hidden Dangers: A Survival Guide for Narcissism, Deception and Betrayal</u>

<u>Relationship Solutions: Effective Strategies to Heal Your Heart and Create the Happiness you Deserve</u>

<u>The Emotionally Destructive Marriage</u>

<u>The Journey: A Roadmap for Self-Healing after Narcissistic Abuse</u>

<u>Boundaries</u>

References

Ashar, Y. K., Andrews-Hanna, J. R., Dimidjian, S., & Wager, T. D. (2017, June 21). *Empathic Care and Distress: Predictive Brain Markers and Dissociable Brain Systems*. Neuron. https://www.ncbi.nlm.nih.gov/pmc/articles/PMC5532453/.

BBC. *A cultural history of gaslighting*. BBC Culture. https://www.bbc.com/culture/article/20191122-cultural-history-of-gaslighting-in-film.

BPD Central. - BPD Central. (2017). http://www.bpdcentral.com/faq/personality-disorders.

Brazier, Y. (2020, September 29). *Narcissistic personality disorder: Symptoms, diagnosis, and treatment*. Medical News Today. https://www.medicalnewstoday.com/articles/9741.

Bree Bonchay, L. C. S. W. (2017, June 1). *Narcissistic Abuse Affects Over 158 Million People in the U.S.* Psych Central. https://psychcentral.com/lib/narcissistic-abuse-affects-over-158-million-people-in-the-u-s.

Cain, D. (2014, March 16). *Your Lifestyle Has Already Been Designed*. Thought Catalog. https://thoughtcatalog.com/david-cain/2013/01/your-lifestyle-has-already-been-designed/.

Current World Population. Worldometer. (2020). https://www.worldometers.info/world-population/.

Eschner, K. (2017, August 23). *The Six-Day Hostage Standoff That Gave Rise to 'Stockholm Syndrome'*. Smithsonian.com. https://www.smithsonianmag.com/smart-news/six-day-hostage-standoff-gave-rise-stockholm-syndrome-180964537/.

Freleng, F. (2018). *Hyde and Hare*. Looney Tunes Wiki. https://looneytunes.fandom.com/wiki/Hyde_and_Hare.

Greenberg, E. (2019, August 3). *10 Stages in the Treatment of Narcissistic Disorders*. Psychology Today. https://www.psychologytoday.com/us/blog/understanding-narcissism/201908/10-stages-in-the-treatment-narcissistic-disorders.

Hammond, C. (2015, May 27). *How Narcissists Use Money to Abuse*. Psych Central. https://www.psychcentral.com/pro/exhausted-woman/2015/05/how-narcissists-use-money-to-abuse#1.

Health, F. B. (Ed.). (2020, August 13). *The Three Clusters of Personality Disorders: Behavioral Health*. Behavioral Health Florida. https://www.behavioralhealthflorida.com/blog/three-clusters-personality-disorders/.

Home. Lifeline. https://suicidepreventionlifeline.org/.

Jack, C. (2020, March 25). The Day You Discover You're a Victim of Narcissistic Abuse. Psychology Today. https://www.psychologytoday.com/us/blog/women-autism-spectrum-disorder/202003/the-day-you-discover-youre-victim-narcissistic-abuse.

Lambert, C. (2018, September 11). *Abused Women Are Not Copependent and Here's Why*. Lambert, C. (2018, September 11). Abused Women Are Not Codependent and Here's Why. Retrieved from https://www.psychologytoday.com/intl/blog/mind-games/201809/abused-women-are-not-codependent-and-heres-why.

Leonard, J. (2019, October 21). *Cognitive dissonance: Definition, effects, and examples*. Medical News Today. https://www.medicalnewstoday.com/articles/326738#overview.

MacMillan, A. (2018, March 23). *How to Spot 'Love Bombing,' a Sneaky Form of Emotional Abuse*. Health.com. https://www.health.com/relationships/love-bombing-emotional-abuse.

Minimizing: A Form of Control. Freedom From Narcissistic and Emotional Abuse. (2017, February 2). https://freedomfromnarcissisticandemotionalabuse.weebly.com/blog/minimizing-a-form-of-control.

Mitchell, J. (2017, January 29). *Most dangerous time for battered women? When they leave.* Ledger. https://www.clarionledger.com/story/news/2017/01/28/most-dangerous-time-for-battered-women-is-when-they-leave-jerry-mitchell/96955552/.

Ni, P. (2018, July 29). *5 Ways Narcissists Compensate for Their Inferiority.* Psychology Today. https://www.psychologytoday.com/us/blog/communication-success/201807/5-ways-narcissists-compensate-their-inferiority.

Pedersen, T. (2013, July 6). *Narcissists' Lack of Empathy Tied to Less Gray Matter.* Psych Central. https://psychcentral.com/news/2013/07/06/narcissists-lack-of-empathy-tied-to-less-gray-matter.

Poston, D. L. (2020, January 2). *3 ways that the U.S. population will change over the next decade.* PBS. https://www.pbs.org/newshour/nation/3-ways-that-the-u-s-population-will-change-over-the-next-decade.

Saeed, K. (2020, February 9). *Can a Narcissist Change If They Really Want To?* Kim Saeed: Narcissistic Abuse Recovery Program. https://kimsaeed.com/2016/08/08/hope-narcissist-can-will-change/.

Smith, B. L. (2020, December 5). In *Propaganda.* Britannica. https://www.britannica.com/topic/propaganda.

Top 10 Favorite Narcissistic Characters. Random Ramblings of a Demented Doorknob. (2010, October 7). http://dementeddoorknob.blogspot.com/2010/10/top-10-favorite-narcissistic-characters.html.

Tudor, H. G. (2020, August 1). *The 5 Reasons the Narcissist Devalues You.* HG Tudor - Knowing The Narcissist - The World's No.1 Resource About Narcissism. https://narcsite.com/2020/08/01/the-5-reasons-the-narcissist-devalues-you-8/.

White, W. (2018, June 12). *The Love Bomb: What is Love Bombing & Why Does It Matter?* ReGain. https://www.regain.us/advice/love/the-love-bomb-what-is-love-bombing-why-does-it-matter/.

Wikimedia Foundation. (2020, November 15). *Cluster B personality disorders*. Wikipedia. https://en.wikipedia.org/wiki/Cluster_B_personality_disorders.

Wikimedia Foundation. (2020, November 30). *Dr. Jekyll and Mr. Hyde (character)*. Wikipedia. https://en.wikipedia.org/wiki/Dr._Jekyll_and_Mr._Hyde_(character).

Wikimedia Foundation. (2021, January 3). *Gaslight (1944 film)*. Wikipedia. https://en.wikipedia.org/wiki/Gaslight_(1944_film).